Charla Pereau with **Joyce Lundholm**

ISBN 0-89877-016-5

Printed in the United States of America

Cover

Scenic Coastline, Baja, California — near the Mission.

I was about to have another baby—someone else's baby.

And I hadn't been designed in heaven to go the motherhood route again: blanket fuzz and spit-up on my best clothes, diaper bags, sleepless nights of feedings and sleepy days of propping up my droopy eyelids with one hand and sterilizing baby bottles with the other.

"Mrs. Pereau, are you happy with your son?"

I looked into the sensitive eyes of the little teenage Indian mother, saw how much the right answer meant to her and quickly replied:

"Yes. He's very handsome."

Her anxiety melted away. "Then I leave you responsible only to God for his care."

It was so touching a remark I had a problem holding back tears.

Charla

Charla's CHILDREN

ACKNOWLEDGEMENTS

"To God be the glory, great things He has done."

I It is with affection and gratitude I hereby acknowledge our staff in Colonia Guerrero, Mexico, past and present who have served the Lord Jesus Christ sacrificially, often without recognition.

II "Plans fail for lack of council, but with many advisors, they succeed." Proverbs 15:22. Our success can be credited in part to the board of directors of the non-profit Foundation for His Ministry. They patiently endure marathon board meetings and give their best.

III Only eternity will reveal what has been accomplished by our network of intercessors who have committed to pray for us daily.

IV Without the encouragement of our spiritual advisor and friend, Pastor John Lucas of Calgary, Alberta, Canada, and Joyce Lundholm who did much of the rewriting and Lu Ann White, my secretary, this manuscript would have been hopelessly buried beneath a mountain of papers on my kitchen table.

V It would take another book to thank all the individuals who have made significant contributions to His Ministry by dollars, household goods, food and work (that is always needed). To those unnamed givers to His Ministry, you will receive rewards in heaven. But it is entirely appropriate that I take this opportunity to thank you in Jesus' name.

Charla Pereau
FOUNDATION FOR HIS MINISTRY
Box 9803
North Hollywood, CA 91609

All proceeds from this book have been assigned to His Ministry.

Canadian address:
MARANATHA EVANGELISTIC ASSOCIATION
P.O. Box 1292
Calgary, Alberta, Canada T2P 2L2

Photos in this book were taken by Vicki Hesterman, Dave Emery and Jay Bertelsen

DEDICATION

To my mother, Olive Hanna Warren Thayer, who has always been my prime supporter. Her guiding principle was, "It's always too soon to quit. When the way is steep or rough you just keep on walking." And to Chuck, my beloved best friend and faithful partner in His Ministry. It is our prayer this will benefit His little ones in Mexico.

OLIVE HANNAH WARREN THAYER

THE PEREAU FAMILY IN 1980 (LEFT TO RIGHT): COLLEEN ANDREA PEREAU LOMBARD, CRAIG BRADLEY PEREAU, CHARLES DANA PEREAU, CHARLA DAVIS PEREAU, CHARLES DANA PEREAU, SR., CHARLES CURTIS PEREAU, GREGORY BARRETT.

CONTENTS

1

DANGER!

We were in Trouble. The road was a mass of axlebreaking potholes and jagged rocks. We dared not look down — a thousand feet below was the valley and there was no shoulder to protect us.

When we most needed speed to find our destination with the little light left, we had to inch along at five miles an hour or less. Daylight suddenly became twilight in the desolate Baja countryside. The sun, the needle of our gas gauge and our morale were all dangerously low. Our map had given us a false sense of security, showing a number of towns along the little-traveled road. The "towns" were actually tiny fishing hamlets, old mission ruins or isolated adobe huts. There wasn't a gas station in sight.

More than three hundred miles from home, we were lost somewhere on the Baja peninsula. Our families had expected us to be home by now, and there were no phones or radios to contact them or call for help. The fast-approaching darkness, our nearly empty gas tanks, and the fear of Mexican bandits, who were rumored to terrorize the Baja roads, were enough to bring on panic. We tried to stay calm as my husband Chuck gripped the steering wheel and inched along the rutty road.

"What in the world have I gotten us into now?" I asked myself.

A powerful force had attracted me to look for the Mexican village of Colonia Vicente Guerrero, starting with a fascinating article about the place in a newspaper delivered to our North Hollywood, California home. An Episcopalian priest on an historic pilgrimage to the ruins of Spanish missions had stumbled upon some old, abandoned buildings, including a two-story, unfinished motion picture theater, a casino and a motel-brothel in this remote village in Baja California, Mexico. In my Rand McNally Atlas, I had noted how Baja (lower) California jutted away from California like a sharp stalactite, the Gulf of California on its east and the Pacific Ocean on its west. Mainland Mexico was east of the Gulf of California.

I felt compelled to pray for this little village that was 100 years back in time, with no electricity, telephones or other modern conveniences. The town was 180 miles south of the border. We lived 120 miles north of the border.

"A nice day's trip," I had thought.

"Nice" was hardly the word for our trip.

I had suggested to Chuck that we and our close friends Roy and Nell Bean should drive down to Baja on a Saturday morning for a celebration of Chuck's birthday. Chuck is always ready for an outing, and Roy and Nell seldom had the opportunity, so everybody had been willing. We knew next to nothing about Mexico or the terrible conditions of the roads in 1966. Enchanted with the scenic glories of Baja, as many varieties of green cactus and brown and gold chaparral decorated the sandy desert hills and the blue Pacific sparkled on our right, it took us awhile to face reality. There were no towns. There were no gas stations. We were in trouble.

Now it was really dark, and no one was speaking to me. Did such a place as Colonia Vicente Guerrero even exist?

"How could God have me pray for this village if there wasn't such a place?" I asked the silent group in self-defense.

"I don't know about that," replied Chuck grimly as the headlights speared a pile of rocks ahead. "But, sister, you better start praying now, because we're almost out of gas and lost somewhere on the Baja peninsula."

The time before midnight never seemed more black in my life. We hadn't seen a sign of life for hours. As we inched along over what didn't even seem a road, we were all more concerned than we wanted to admit. I thought about our family in North Hollywood. We had expected to be back home at about this time. So had Roy and Nell. Our children and the babysitter would be worried sick. All the while, we felt helpless, traveling farther away, not knowing where we were or where we were going.

I dared not look at the gas gauge. By this time the motor had to be running only on high octane prayer. Then we crossed over a rock-littered, dry riverbed and the headlights caught something in the beam: a few adobe huts. We were able to make out a small white stucco adobe building. Straining our eyes, we finally could distinguish lettering on its front, "Informacion."

"See the sign," cried Chuck. "That's got to mean information!" Outside the structure which appeared to be a cantina, we saw a small slender man in dark clothing.

Through the open window, Chuck and I, leaning over the steering wheel, tried to convey that we were lost and needed gasoline and could he help us. After endless unsuccessful efforts to communicate, we appeared to make a breakthrough. He directed us with gestures, but when he saw that we didn't understand, he indicated he wanted to get in. I moved over, and he slid into the seat beside me.

"What an angel he is to come with us," I commented to Chuck. Our guide led us down what seemed to be a sandy trail. Suddenly in the starlight, we could see the faint outline of several large buildings.

The man indicated we should stop near one of the structures, and when we did, he got out and rapped at the door. For almost five minutes he persisted and finally, the door opened. There, in a crimson bathrobe, stood a Mexican woman in her fifties — brown-eyed and brown-haired, with a broad, five foot two, 180-pound frame.

For a short time the man talked, occasionally gesturing toward us, apparently telling the woman the dilemma of the lost Americans. She nodded her head all the while and, looking toward the car, hand-waved for us to come in.

After all the suspenseful hours on the road, we found relief in the woman's welcome. Suddenly, we became aware of how exhausted we were. Never had such a plain woman looked so beautiful as did this Mexican woman to us weary travelers. In fluent, Spanish-accented English, she invited us in, introduced herself as Juana and told us she was from the United States.

"I can put you up for the night," she said. "In the morning I can help you."

Almost in unison, Chuck and I remembered the man who had so considerately guided us to shelter. In the open door, we turned to thank him.

No one was there!

We peered down the road but could see no one.

Genial and cooperative, Juana introduced us to her son, a black-haired, macho young fellow in his mid-twenties, who lived with her. "We have nine homeless children staying here in the old Casino building," she informed us. My interest perked up.

She offered us chairs in the snug warmth of a large, kitchen-dining room area and then, noting our fatigue, said, "But you are tired and would probably like to sleep."

How could we sleep without having the foremost question in our minds answered? So I asked it, "Do you know where we can buy gasoline around here?"

Juana smiled, showing irregular, white teeth.

"I have all you need."

Juana opened a door to an adjoining room and, with her son, hauled out two, double-bed mattresses and blankets for us to sleep on the floor.

Whatever sleep I had was fitful and brief. Distress hounded me. I knew that the children and our friends would be worried that we had had an accident and with no telephones in the area, we couldn't call to relieve their anxiety. Rather than toss and turn and disturb Chuck, I got up just before dawn, dressed and walked outside with my troubles.

In the pinkish light of dawn, I wandered over the property, praying for a solution to our problem. Then I was overcome by the eerie beauty of the place — the deteriorating buildings, the powdery beige sand, pinos, palms and a pepper tree, all muted with fine dust against a distant slab of red mountain.

As I looked toward the mountain, the first verse of Psalm 121 came to mind: "I will lift up mine eyes unto the hills, from whence cometh my help?"

Why someone had constructed these buildings in

the sparsely populated area of Baja California was a mystery to me. If they were the ones I had read about in the newspaper article, one was a gambling casino, the second was a single-story, L-shaped motel-brothel, and the third building was a huge cement block motion picture theater. The old theater was an unusual shape; it made me think of an enormous grey elephant at rest.

Until that morning, I knew little about visions, probably because I had never had one. As I studied the old abandoned motel — its weatherbeaten doors sagging wearily on rusted hinges and smooth drifts of light-colored sand inside — I heard sounds of children laughing.

How could that be? Obviously the building was empty. I stepped inside and saw that, indeed, no one was there. But it came again — the distinct sound of children laughing. There was no mistake.

Then the red salt-weed, the cream-colored white blossoms on the wild gourd, and the bunches of wild grass seemed to disappear and in their place came a waving field of grain. A verse from the Bible almost lit up my mind: "Lo, the fields are white unto the harvest, but the laborers are few."

All at once it came to me — "Lord," I whispered in awe, "This place must be meant for a home for needy children."

I walked over the entire 72 acres of flat land and felt a powerful, spine-tingling urge, which I obeyed, "Lord, I claim this property for this purpose in Your name!"

Surely someone would be raised up who could make this vision come true. I prayed for this to happen, never dreaming that I, a housewife from North Hollywood, California, would be that someone.

Now dawn's pinkness gave way to brighter

daylight and I headed back to the building where the Mexican woman, Juana, had graciously given us lodging at midnight. I was just in time to sit down to a breakfast of beans and tortillas with Chuck and our friends. After explaining my absence, I said, "Judging from what I've seen, this must be Colonia Vicente Guerrero."

Juana nodded verification, and Chuck, Roy and Nell requested that I give them a walking tour of the property once we finished eating.

I did, telling them of my unique experience at the old motel. Just as our sightseeing appeared to be finished, we became curious about a small, flat-roofed, ugly frame building across the road, its whitewashed laths hammered on crookedly. Something strange then happened, convincing me for all times that God inhabits places other than just beautiful edifices with stained glass splendor.

Opening the double-door to enter, we could not step inside. It was as if a powerful force stood between us and the dark interior. Never before had I experienced such a strong, supernatural presence.

"This place is filled with angels," said Roy Bean in a hushed, reverential voice.

Now the resisting force eased off, and we quietly went in. Slowly our eyes adapted, and we made out a little wooden altar in the front. A kerosene lamp gave off faint illumination and the odor of burning oil. Nine children were kneeling at the altar in prayer.

As we sat in the back on rickety old theater seats, the atmosphere was awesome, I felt strangly moved to go forward and lay hands on these children and pray, but I held back. I didn't know Spanish, and, besides, why would I do such a thing?

Despite my reluctance, I was drawn to the front

and laid hands on them.

"God, bring protection to these little ones in Jesus' name," I prayed. "Bring illumination and the person of Jesus to each of them."

Suddenly seven of them began speaking in languages of the Spirit. I had not noticed that Juana had quietly come in. Then one of the boys — a teenager whose name I learned later was Pedro — began talking above the others in fervent, inspired Spanish.

"It is a prophecy," cried a surprised Juana and, almost automatically, she interpreted for us. Pedro, biblically ignorant, like the others at the altar, spoke impassioned words from Isaiah 61:1:

"The Spirit of the Lord God is upon me; because the Lord hath anointed me to preach good tidings unto the meek; he hath sent me to bind up the brokenhearted, to proclaim liberty to the captives, and the opening of the prison to them that are bound . . .".

A thrill made my flesh tingle. Obviously, God had anointed him to be a preacher of the gospel. We were all stricken dumb with the working of the Holy Spirit and the majesty of the moment. It was as if we had shared a confidence with God — not merely to know His intentions for Pedro but to serve as God's earthly assistants to help Pedro move into God's will for him.

When Pedro had finished, I whispered to Chuck, more loudly than I realized: "I believe we're supposed to take him home with us."

Chuck's glance told me he agreed. Over our seventeen years together we had developed appreciation and respect for each other's sensitivity to God's leading.

Juana, recognizing the uniqueness of the Holy

Spirit's manifestation, vigorously nodded approval, her fleshy chins bobbing up and down.

"Pedro came to us lost and alone a few weeks ago," Juana explained. "He couldn't stand what was going on at home. His father, a soldier on an army base near Ensenada and an alcoholic, sold his mother into prostitution to other soldiers."

For an instant Juana observed our shocked expressions, then continued: "There's something unusual about his coming here. Most runaways head north, toward Tijuana or the United States. He came south, was kicked by a horse near our road, injured and brought to us by a passing good Samaritan. Quite a coincidence that you should meet him here."

"God's coincidence," I commented and immediately began thinking about taking him home with us. *"How is this going to work out?"* I asked myself. *"The youth speaks no English."* Then it occurred to me, *"God has led us to him. He will handle the language problem."*

Chuck broke into my thoughts, "Charla, let's get the boy ready and head for home. We've got to get back to the family. They and the baby-sitter will be worried sick about us. Besides, I don't want to drive those hairpin, mountain turns and rock-strewn excuses for roads in the dark again."

Roy and Nell seconded the motion. Juana invited us to tank up the car from a large drum on top of two tall sawhorses. After filling up, paying for the gasoline and thanking her for that and her hospitality, we pulled out. Pedro, timid and somewhat frightened, was in the front seat between Chuck and me.

We couldn't communicate with him, and the farther we went, the more I wondered if we had been impractical — even foolhardy — in taking him with us. Yet I also remembered how we had been completely convicted by the Holy Spirit and that we were acting in faith. God would help us.

As we traveled, Roy commented, "The trip north by daylight certainly beats the hair-raiser we had last night." We all laughed.

As Chuck drove, concentrating fully on the bad road — bumps, potholes, rocks and thrilling twists and turns with sheer dropoffs — I knew that the creases on his forehead were not caused only by complete attention to driving. Like me, he was wondering how we were going to get Pedro over the border.

After all, we knew next to nothing about immigration laws, had no birth certificate or any legal papers for him. What would we do if the immigration officers refused to admit him to the United States? Would we have to take him all that way back?

The closer we came to Tijuana, the less confidence I had. *"Why had I suggested bringing Pedro back with us?"* I kept asking myself, *"How in the world did you get wound up in this Mexico business anyhow?"*

2

INVOLVEMENT—WHO NEEDS IT?

It all began in the summer of '61 at the Lutheran Family Bible Camp at pine-scented Camp Seeley in the San Bernardino mountains, an hour's drive from Los Angeles, and about as different from the barren sands of Baja as it could be.

In that beautiful, natural setting, it always seemed that God was very near. The relaxed schedule gave us time to develop more than surface relationships. Worship was less formal than the traditional, liturgical services at home. I was prepared for the pleasure of talking with old friends like Audrey and Dave Taylor (owner of North Drug of Costa Mesa) and for a time of refreshing, revitalizing and renewing in God. I got that and more.

First of all, Chuck and I became even more attached to the Taylors. It was a real inspiration to be with them because they radiated Christian love and we felt a true fellowship with them — Audrey, a lovely lady with dark hair and a ready smile and Dave, a tall, slender man who would have hugged the whole world if he could have gotten his arms around it.

Like Chuck and I, the Taylors had a first-born daughter named Andrea, something that made us feel even closer. Audrey and Dave had a zeal for missions and unusual generosity. Tithing was just a launching pad for giving money and themselves to Christian causes. I have never seen a couple with such a zeal for sharing Christ with the lost.

A family with four children of school age came to camp with a little Korean orphan from an adoption agency. The Caucasian children and their Oriental sister blended well and I felt happy and warm all over.

"That's wonderful," I whispered to Chuck, not fully understanding my emotions. I was pretty much self-contained at the time and not given to showing my feelings. I had no idea then that this family's deed, plus my mother's lifelong policy of having room for one more in our home, would serve as a pattern for us.

Two more things happened that made us know our lives would never again be the same — one through a slow and subtle process and the other through a spiritual earthquake.

New Bible insights, moving talks by ministers, spirited group singing and prayers influenced us. Then, as if a shaft of heavenly, white light had beamed into our minds, we saw the kind of Christians we were and the kind we ought to be.

Nobody had been busier in church work than Chuck and I. Every time the church doors opened, we were there. We had been locked into "churchianity," rather than Christianity. Somehow, unknowingly, we had pulled the plug and lost vital contact with Jesus the person. We were living in a ministry, rather than letting our lives be a ministry, a revelation of Jesus.

Suddenly we realized that Christ is more concerned with who we are than with what we do. We prayed for a new spiritual dimension. We rededicated our lives to the Lord in a fresh, pure, new way. We asked that Christ's life be manifested through us. It was a mountaintop experience.

All was too serene to stay that way.

One cool, quiet night under the flickering stars, 250 of us sat on benches in prayer around a campfire. Golden flames lit up our faces.

Outside the clearing, in the mysterious shadows, hundreds of majestic pines towered over us. A breeze made rustling music with their needles — soothing accompaniment to the soft murmur of our prayers. Like the others, I was enchanted — in tune with nature and in perfect communication with God.

Then, with no warning, the woman next to me sprang to her feet. In a nerve-shattering, almost hysterical voice, she began crying out in a strange, exotic language.

What was happening? In the firelight, she didn't appear to be ill. I was shocked. What kind of Lutheran would make such an outburst?

One of the ministers, a large, grey-haired man, hurried past the fire toward her. He laid a paternal hand on her shoulder, silenced her, and pronounced a formal benediction, as if nothing irregular had happened. Then he authoritatively announced, "You are dismissed. Please go to your cabins!"

Go to our cabins? How ridiculous!

As he led her away, pandemonium broke loose — confusion, puzzlement, antagonism.

"Is she crazy?" someone questioned.

"I'm not exposing *my* kids to this hysteria again," exclaimed one mother.

"Either she leaves this camp or we do!" cried a

man.

"What's bugging her?" another voice inquired.

Noting our confusion, one of the pastors called out:

"Attention. Give me your attention. We will all assemble in the chapel. Bring your Bibles!"

I couldn't wait.

Together, two of the ministers talked to us for a half-hour about Bible references to the Baptism in the Holy Spirit and the supernatural gifts.

"This woman was using one of these gifts," explained one of the ministers. "She was speaking in tongues, just as so many did at Pentecost."

The other ministers nodded in agreement.

My Irish temper flared.

Everybody knew that the manifestations of the Holy Spirit mentioned in the Book of Acts had disappeared after the first century A.D.

I was so mad I heard only a fraction of the ridiculous dialogue.

" . . . We, as a camp, must not scorn this woman whose behavior was so unusual. We must unite in open love for her . . . ".

That made me burn. Unite in love for *her*?

I couldn't buy this "tongues" business. After all, I was a well-grounded Sunday school teacher and knew a little about the Bible, too. "Tongues" was not very Lutheran. As a matter of fact, it was not very *anything.*

Even after our return home, I was upset and couldn't wait to report this disturbing incident to my own beloved pastor.

"Pastor, you wouldn't believe the bizarre thing that happened at Camp Seeley . . . ". I unreeled the story in self-righteous indignation as if he had been to blame for it.

He listened quietly for a few minutes:

"Charla, there are many members of our congregation who have had the gift of tongues and other gifts of the Spirit for more than ten years . . .".

I was stunned.

"Without exception, these people have assumed leadership positions in the church, are noted Bible teachers and humble servants who love the Lord and bear the fruits of the Spirit. A good number of Lutheran pastors have recently had this experience. You've heard of Larry Christenson's position?"

I hadn't heard of Larry Christenson, let alone his position.

"No," I replied.

Patiently he appraised me.

"Charla, study the Scripture on this subject and make love your aim."

That love business again!

I thanked him and left in frustration.

Somewhere, somehow, I would show these well-meaning but misguided individuals how utterly wrong they were. The chance came earlier than expected.

In Tuesday's mail, I found an invitation from our church homebuilder's group to a family beach party in San Pedro. The special speaker was to be the Reverend Larry Christenson.

Following an afternoon of good fellowship and fun — swimming, Frisbees, and chicken sandwiches complete with sand — came my big chance to confront Pastor Christenson.

"Pastor." He turned to me. Immediately I was disconcerted. This man was not a wild-eyed heretic, dominating or opinionated. His eyes were full of a melting love. "I understand you speak in tongues."

"Yes," he smiled a white-toothed, warm smile. "The Lord has given me this special dimension of spiritual prayer."

"Do you understand what you are praying?"

"No."

Now he was cornered.

"Then of what earthly value is it?"

"It's not earthly at all. It's spiritual communion with God. My spirit can pray, free of confused reasoning and prejudice."

"I understand you're encouraging this movement."

He nodded vigorously. "One can hardly compare the Book of Acts with a recent history of Christianity without asking, 'Where is the power?' Has the Holy Spirit withdrawn from His dynamic manifestations or have we quenched His free operation by our unbelief?

"I look to the day when His blessings will be sought and received by people in all our Lutheran churches — clergy and laity alike — that we might become His more perfect witnesses."

What he said had a reasonable ring, but I was still not convinced. Like all the rest, he was deluded. Soon I would prove that.

For three months, I wore ruts between home, the public and church libraries, and UCLA — trying to find the truth, which, I hoped, would expose the blindness and folly of the Christensons of this world.

I read everything available on the baptism, infilling and gifts of the Holy Spirit. The pages of Acts, Corinthians and Ephesians in my Bible were worn thin. Many notable, modern theologians shared my position, and I sent up rockets of joy. One of my favorite radio ministers sounded off frequently on the evils of the charismatic renewal. I added his booklets on the subject to my growing stockpile of ammunition.

Six of my women friends who had expressed an interest in the gifts of the Holy Spirit got a tongue-lashing from me and the full brunt of my research.

One day I read something that rocked me. Many of the early saints had had supernatural gifts and visitations long after the first century church. Even worse was information in *Sour's History of the Christian Church.* The founder of our church, Martin Luther, was a "speaker of tongues and interpreter in one person, endowed with all the gifts of the Spirit."

"Oh, no," I groaned. "Martin Luther, how could you have done this to me?"

The words of his well-known hymn, *A Mighty Fortress is our God,* had wandered through my mind frequently without making much of an impression, but now a certain line kept repeating:

"The Spirit and the gifts are ours through Him who with us sideth . . .".

Could I be wrong? So many times I had been. That night I prayed, *"Dear Lord, if these things are true, I've been blinded by my prejudice, depending upon my reason and the knowledge of man. God, help me. If You have more for me, I'll receive it."*

Like the gifts of the Spirit, miracles were supposed to be limited to no later than the first century A.D., while Jesus was on earth, I thought. But hadn't He given us the Holy Spirit, the Comforter, in His place? And would the third member of the Holy Trinity be less powerful and able than the others?

I wondered about these things as I read Catherine Marshall's classic *Beyond Ourselves.* Many miraculous stories in it left an indelible impression on me, particularly one about Dr. William Standish Reed, who couples prayer with the practice of medicine.

A case which specialists had given up as lost was turned over to him. Fifteen-year-old Karen Emmott, of Oklahoma City, had been in a coma for weeks, suffered brain damage, partially paralyzed lungs and was sentenced by physicians to the rest of her life as a vegetable.

Dr. Reed laid hands on her, prayed and set a program of prayer and positive thinking and speaking for her parents visiting her hospital room.

Karen's complete recovery is one of the great physical miracles of all times and renewed my faith that the power and miracles of Jesus had not disappeared. I thought of Hebrews 13:8: "Jesus Christ, the same yesterday and today and forever."

Then I got so thoroughly tangled up in a series of incredible happenings that, for a while, I lost sight of miracles and "gifts".

3

A BATTLE OF WILLS

A few weeks after Bible Camp, a small item in our church bulletin almost jumped off the page at me:

"The Lutheran Mission in Oaxaca, Mexico needs a home for a teenage Indian girl."

As I sat in church, I thought, "*Maybe we could take in a teenage Indian girl.*" Ever since Chuck and I had been married, our home — like that of my parents — had been open to those who needed help or sanctuary. This was just a natural part of being a Christian. It was hard for me to remember a time when we hadn't had an expanded family. Even now Chuck's and my boys, Dana and Craig, shared a bedroom with my nephew Dick, who had lived with us since 1957. Colleen Andrea had a room to herself. Perhaps she would be willing to share her room. It was just an idea.

I sent a letter of inquiry to the Oaxaca mission:

"Do you still need a home for a teenage girl?" If so, please send us details. Enclosed is a ten dollar donation. May God continue to bless your work."

Two months later, a letter arrived from a Pastor Harold Moench, the minister of a Lutheran Church in San Antonio, Texas. My eyes froze on one sentence:

"Would you consider adopting a yet-to-be-born Zapotec Indian baby from Oaxaca, Mexico . . .?"

I stared at the letter.

What an unorthodox way of placing unwanted children into homes! You send them a ten-dollar donation, and they offer a free sample.

A certain expression in the letter baffled and bothered me:

"We were led to write you . . .".

It was probably one of those churchy terms of other denominations. In any event, it got under my fingernails. Supposedly God had done the leading. I showed Chuck the letter and watched the expression in his blue eyes. My husband had a heart the size of Texas, so I shouldn't have expected him to react as I had.

"Maybe we ought to pray and ask God about this," he said.

"No way," I snapped. "This is one I don't need to pray about." Craig had just gone into the first grade, and my daytime was liberated. "A baby — really!" Right at Chuck's feet, the linoleum had buckled. "We need new floor-covering. And that washing machine sounds like 'The Anvil Chorus'. We've got to have a new one."

Stinging tears began to form in my eyes. That night the sun went down on an armed truce, at least on my part.

I couldn't get that letter off my mind and started doing some wishful thinking. Could it possibly have come from a phony organization? Next day, I showed it to our pastor, hoping he would tell me to forget it.

"No, Charla, there's nothing wrong here," he responded. "This is a legitimate mission. I know of this minister."

My keen disappointment must have shown, because he said, "Charla, have you prayed about this request?"

"I don't need to. I know this is not God's will for us."

Seeing that I wasn't open to suggestion, he said, "I'll run a note in next Sunday's bulletin, and see if we'll get a response."

I stifled a sigh of relief.

Meanwhile, I had to answer the letter, and I couldn't put in writing my many fears. How would our parents and other relatives react to an Indian infant? After all, they were from a generation in which prejudice was often tolerated. We had told none of them about our correspondence with the mission. How would the baby be received in our predominantly Norwegian Lutheran congregation?

Then my mind switched to other considerations. Would the child be free from defects? Could I love him or her as my very own? How could the mother possibly give up her child for adoption? This sort of sacrifice was inconceivable to me.

Cutting off my negative self-questioning, I penned the letter, listing every acceptable objection I could think of to adopting the baby. I was sure we wouldn't be able to pass the California regulations for adoption of a child, our monthly school tuition for four children was high, and we didn't have enough rooms in the house.

"That's that," I told myself exultantly, as I dropped the letter into the mailbox.

It wasn't.

Soon I received a second letter, this time from a Mrs. C. G. Shawd, a member of Pastor Moench's congregation in San Antonio.

"I have been praying and feel led of the Lord to

write you to prayerfully consider taking this baby."

That made me angry. What right did someone else have to "feel led" about *my* life? Why didn't she feel led to adopt the baby herself? What colossal nerve to dictate God's will in my life!

Ruth Marshall, a dear friend who had seen the first letter, read the second. "You know, Charla, I, too, have an inner knowing that somehow it is God's will for you to have that baby."

I glanced at her like Julius Caesar must have at his friend Brutus after being stabbed by him. From that day, every time I saw her, I took off in the opposite direction.

Once my antagonism cooled down, I began to wonder what God's will actually was in this matter. On Sunday in church as the entire congregation prayed the Lord's prayer, we got to the words, "Thy will be done," and they stuck in my throat.

I seemed to be involved in a sub-surface battle with God. Often I would choke up and cry, fearful of God and His will. Where did I fit into God's will? Where was the line between that and my free will? I had to talk to someone and spilled out everything to Marge, our pastor's wife. A mother of five, she wore contemporary clothing and was warm, outgoing, colorful and understanding. Her Bible wisdom was sound, and she was a brilliant writer of books and screenplays.

"Have you ever been out of God's will, Charla?"

"Yes."

"What's it like out there?"

"It's hell."

"Charla, do you believe God is love?"

"Yes."

"Do you believe that God desires only good in your life?"

"I . . . I don't know."

She let me think that over. I remembered that God is love and that He is our Father.

"Charla, do you consider yourself to be a child of God?"

"Yes."

"If you are truly a child of God, nothing can come into your life that doesn't go by the throne of God, that isn't for your ultimate good. Do you accept that?"

That was certainly biblical.

"Yes. God does desire only good in our lives, although it may not seem good at the time," I replied.

"Can you trust Him and submit your will to Him?"

"Yes."

When I returned home, I knelt down by the living room couch and prayed, *"Lord, if this is truly Your will, make me willing."*

I felt much better coming off my knees than I had going down on them — as if the world had been lifted from my back. My mind was at ease and light as a soap bubble. Obviously, all God wanted me to do was to submit to His will. *"I'm off the hook — free, Praise God!"*

So I thought.

The item the pastor placed in the church bulletin did no good. There were no takers for the baby, but maybe with friendly persuasion, I could find a home for it in our congregation. I riffled through the church directory. Many people I knew didn't have children. After thirty phone calls, I realized why. They didn't have them, because they didn't want them.

Then came an inspiration.

"The Downings would be just right."

They had recently adopted a racially-mixed eighteen-month old baby, after having waited eighteen years.

I dialed.

In less than a minute, my inspiration plummeted to dejection. One infant was all they could handle.

God's will seemed to be for me to write a quick letter to San Antonio.

". . . If you positively cannot find anyone else for this baby, we will take it."

That was as far as I could go. Surely, God would provide a more suitable home than ours. I felt at peace with myself, the world and God.

Then it happened.

On November 9, 1961, as I was putting dinner on the table, I received a long-distance call from San Antonio. It was Pastor Moench:

"Mrs. Pereau, your son is born."

My son!

I thought I was going to die. A hard knot formed in the pit of my stomach. I fought back tears.

Chuck and the kids were elated.

"What are we going to name him?" Chuck asked, and they began to reel off names.

I felt trapped, as if the kitchen walls were moving in to crush me. If I could only run a thousand miles away and never come back . . . .

I pecked mechanically at my food and excused myself to attend a Sunday school teachers' meeting at church.

As I inserted the key into the car's ignition, I couldn't hold back any longer. I cried until my eyes and face were red and swollen.

"Lord, you called my bluff."

That night convinced me more than anything else

that the Indian baby was indeed in the Lord's will for me. I had no sooner stepped into the meeting room when everyone shouted, "Surprise."

What a surprise!

It was a baby shower for me.

At the forefront of the group were Betty Haaland and Ruth Marshall, who had known from the beginning that this baby was meant for our home. They had taken a step of faith and arranged the baby shower. Was it coincidence that it happened on the very night when we were notified that the infant was ours?

After regrouping my emotions from the shock, I noted that the meeting room looked like a store for baby items — everything anyone would need: bottles, toys, crib, blankets, layette, stroller.

Another *coincidence* that shook me up was the gift of gifts: a small, grey-brown, Navajo Indian purse of ruglike material and bulging with paper money. One hundred and sixty-eight children had contributed a dollar each — Sunday school kids, Campfire Girls and Bluebirds. I was deeply touched.

When I went to pay for my round-trip fare to San Antonio, I was overwhelmed. The cost came to exactly what the children had given me — one hundred and sixty-eight dollars! As the airplane headed toward its destination, my mellow mood changed to uncertainty, then to the stark reality of my situation.

With all our children finally in school all day, I had felt liberated. Now I was about to be tied down again.

I was about to have another baby — someone else's baby.

From my perspective in the year of our Lord 1961, that infant, conceived by an unwed, teenage Zapotec Indian girl in southern Mexico and born in

San Antonio, hadn't been designed in heaven to fit neatly into my set routines of our middle class, Protestant family.

And I hadn't been designed in heaven to go the motherhood route again: blanket fuzz and spit-up on my best clothes, diaper bags, sleepless nights of feedings and sleepy days of propping up my droopy eyelids with one hand and sterilizing baby bottles with the other.

Another grim reality got to me. Inflation was working its disappearing act with the American dollar and our family budget. With $200 a month going out for the children's tuition at a Christian school and unexpected expenses, Chuck's very good salary as a member of the Los Angeles City Fire Department didn't need another hungry mouth to feed.

Yet we had a firm commitment to feed another.

Verses from Matthew 6 popped into my head. I was being anxious about what the Pereau family would eat and drink and with what we would be clothed. Sure enough, the birds of the air didn't sow or reap or gather into barns, and the lilies of the field didn't toil or spin, and the good Lord took care of them.

If I had had the brains of a bird or a lily, I wouldn't have been so concerned, but I was me, a little short of faith, flying at 30,000 feet and near San Antonio.

Why play mental tug of war with myself? I had just enough time to slip into the restroom and freshen up before the stewardess would order us to fasten our seat belts for landing.

The reflection in the mirror before me came as a shock. That oval, unmistakably Irish, twenty-nine year old face now showed something unusual: a forehead full of horizontal worry lines. What was going on inside was showing on the outside.

Even those brown eyes, often bright with amusement, seemed clouded, dull and drawn with concern. I sighed. Mirrors just weren't what they used to be!

Seated once again, buckled in for the landing, I resigned myself. I was going to go through with my commitment.

Now in San Antonio, I was driven by Pastor Moench to the home of Mrs. C. G. Shawd, the church member who was taking care of the infant and his convalescing mother in a guest house in the rear.

An unwelcome question entered my mind. How could Chuck and I possibly pay the cost of the Indian girl's hospitalization and delivery of her baby?

"*Well, God,*" I thought, "*You've got me this far. You're going to have to work it out, as you have other problems in the past.*"

After a brief get-acquainted period with my hostess, I got down to basics. My curiosity was itching for answers.

"What does the baby look like? What were the circumstances of the girl that made adoption of her baby necessary?" I asked.

Mrs. Shawd answered my last question first. She seemed to know that I wouldn't hear a thing once I saw the baby.

A girl in her teens, the mother had come from near Oaxaca, two hundred miles south of Mexico City. A tourist center famous for fine gardens, colonial churches such as Santa Domingo, handwrought gold and silver filigree, black pottery and colorful serapes, this is one of the few cities in Mexico where Indians have stoutly resisted integration with their Spanish conquerors.

Zapotec and Mixtec Indians remain exclusive by living in the low mountains that rim Oaxaca and deal with the Spanish and tourist only to make a living.

Several missions there spread Bible teachings to the Indians and bring them the good news of salvation through Jesus. Guilt-ridden about her pregnancy without a husband, the girl had visited a Lutheran mission to receive the forgiveness and love of God.

She did not want her child to suffer the stigma and persecution of illegitimacy. The girl knew it would be wonderful if her baby could be adopted by a Christian family and given advantages she could not offer. She prayed, and now her prayer was about to be answered.

The missionaries had put her on a bus to San Antonio, where Mrs. Shawd had met her at the bus terminal and driven her home. In her purse was a slip of paper with the name of a Christian woman in North Hollywood, California, who had promised a home for her baby.

Mrs. Shawd had tried to get her into a hospital when her labor pains began, but she was afraid to go and refused. Zapotec Indians had babies at home and convalesced there. The one person she had known who had gone to a hospital had died there. A physician delivered the baby in Mrs. Shawd's home at no charge.

I was relieved. One wide river had been crossed. Before I had asked, it had been answered.

Suddenly, my hostess inquired:

"How would you like to see the baby?"

I could hardly wait. She took me to a nearby bedroom. There he was in a clothes basket under a pink blanket. I glanced down and gasped. His straight, raven black hair was thick and long. He was a bronze color and his face was flat.

"*Dear God,*" I thought, "*He's got a face only a mother could love!*"

Then it hit me. *"I'm* the mother."

I had hardly regained my composure when my hostess asked, "Would you consider meeting his mother?"

Never good at handling scenes, I visualized the young mother having a trauma when she realized she would never again see her son. That would be too emotion-packed for me!

"I can't. I just can't."

Mrs. Shawd put her arm around my shoulder. She seemed to understand, yet she said:

"I wish you would. She's so young, uneasy and frightened about her son. If she could just see you, it would dispel her fears and reservations."

The request was reasonable enough.

"Can't you give her peace of mind, Mrs Pereau?"

"I'll try, Mrs Shawd."

The mother knew I was coming. She would not let me see her in bed, so she dressed and was standing in an ample, white Terry cloth bathrobe when I came in. Just a mite of a girl with long, straight, black hair and almond-shaped, soft, almost black eyes — a classic Indian beauty — she nervously smiled at me.

My hostess had had the foresight to bring in an interpreter, who quickly translated the first thing that Indian girl asked, "Mrs. Pereau, are you happy with your son?"

I looked into her sensitive eyes, saw how much the right answer meant to her, and quickly replied:

"Yes. He's very handsome."

Her anxiety melted away.

"Then I leave you responsible only to God for his care."

It was so touching a remark, I had a problem

holding back tears. She had so much more maturity and was so much more in command of the situation than I.

Wrung out emotionally, I was glad to leave for the airport with my brand new son, cozily wrapped in a pink blanket. On the way, I recalled being cautioned against admitting that the baby was not my own. Certain regulations on adoption prohibited taking a child across state lines until legally adopted.

We missed the plane, and the airline rerouted us on three different aircraft, with a connecting flight from St. Louis to Los Angeles.

On each plane, the stewardess would say, "Oh, let me see your baby."

When I turned back the blanket, she would see the long, jet black hair, bronze skin and flat features, stare speechlessly at the baby and me and back again at the baby. Then she would call over another stewardess and ask, "Would you mind showing her your baby?

I had expected to land in Los Angeles on Saturday morning, but with the rerouting, I came in at night, tired and a little down. What a delight to see faithful Chuck at the gate!

He couldn't wait to take that little bundle into his arms and turn back the cover. He lit up with pleasure.

"Oh, he's beautiful."

I glanced sharply at Chuck and thought: *"He really thinks he's beautiful,"* and my loving appreciation for Chuck grew even more.

Many times he tiptoed to the antique, white, wicker bassinette in the corner of our master bedroom, looked into the low profile face and said, "He's beautiful." It took me months to see what Chuck saw immediately.

A lot of possible names for our new baby had been kicked around on the night that he was born. Craig had said, "His name should be Charles Curtis, because the only Indian who was ever vice-president of the United States was Charles Curtis in the Hoover administration." We all agreed. So Charles Curtis it was. Charles Curtis won instant approval of the whole Pereau family.

CHARLES CURTIS PEREAU WITH MOM AND DAD

4

A BATTLE OF WILLS CONTINUES

A few weeks later, Teddy Matson, my Sunday School Superintendent, phoned me in distress.

"Charla, I've had car trouble, and I'm on my way to a Christian meeting I just can't afford to miss. Can you drive me there and attend with me?"

Comfortable in my own neat little version of traditional Lutheranism, I didn't even know that there were Christian meetings outside the church.

I was pleased to do her the favor. My mother was caring for Charles Curtis. "Sure, I'll take you there. I can wait in the car and work on my Bible correspondence course."

At the Embassy hotel, Teddy insisted I join her. "You'll enjoy the speaker."

"Who's that?"

"Dr. William Standish Reed."

I had just read about him in Catherine Marshall's book. I just *had* to hear him.

Five minutes later, I was sorry. We had just settled in our seats in the huge meeting room when a woman not far from me rose. Out of her mouth came a torrent of words — a crazy rush of some foreign language. When she stopped, a man got to his feet and interpreted.

My first thought was, *"Dear Lord, can't I get away from these kooks?"*

After Dr. Reed's moving message on the integral part of Jesus in his medical career — and some spectacular accounts of healings to illustrate his points — he offered an invitation to those seeking "more of Jesus" to come to the front. Oh, how I longed for more of Him — for additional power to be His effective witness!

Before I realized what was happening, I was in the center aisle, halfway to the front.

"*Why isn't everybody going forward?*" I asked myself in panic. Then I got a blinding flash of reality; I had been trapped into an altar call. I was too embarrassed to turn back.

"Lord, how do I get out of this?"

I couldn't. Ten or eleven of us women and men clustered in a ragged line up front.

Starting at the end opposite me, Dr. Reed, Pastor Harald Bredesen and David duPlessis began praying. One would vigorously lay hands on each person's head and the others on his or her shoulders.

Without fail, everyone began speaking some unknown language. Obviously, Dr. Reed, Pastor Bredesen and David duPlessis were not helping these individuals receive more of Jesus. They were administering the baptism in the Holy Spirit.

That troubled me. I had come forward for exactly what the speaker had promised — "more of Jesus" — not the new-to-me manifestations of the Holy Spirit. At that time, it didn't occur to me that one can't separate the baptism of the Holy Spirit from Jesus Christ, for through the Holy Spirit we receive power to witness unto Him.

Another consideration — this one minor — concerned me. I had just had a budget-unbalancing, new hair-style, teased high with every strand lacquered into place.

Now they had worked down to the man next to me. Someone placed hands on his head. Deep gutteral sounds issued from his throat.

I had rehearsed a speech about how the altar call had been misrepresented. Sure, I wanted more of Jesus. I was already born again, but I was not seeking all the gifts of the Holy Spirit.

Now I began my protest. Nobody was listening. The strong hands of Pastor Bredesen clamped down on my crowning glory and flattened it.

Nothing spiritual happened. I was terribly self-conscious, as if a theater spotlight had caught me in its beam. I could feel the eyes of the audience staring at the back of my head. Everybody seemed hanging in silent suspense to see what would happen to me.

A frightening thought jarred me. The speaker and the ministers were going to stand there and pray over me until I spoke in tongues. Silently, I cried out, *"Dear God in Heaven. I do want everything you wish to give me. Please help me!"*

He did.

Some words I had never before heard or spoken tumbled out of my mouth. I felt not even a hint of emotion.

"Thank you, Jesus," I whispered under my breath.

As I left for my seat, I heard an announcement that a similar program would be held that evening for those who couldn't attend by day. This time Pastor Bredesen, a former Lutheran minister, would be the main speaker, aided by Dr. Reed.

On the way home, I was silent. Dr. Reed's testimony, the music, the peculiar, unfamiliar words which I had spoken at the altar kept running around in my head. My prejudice and fears about the gifts of the Holy Spirit seemed to be evaporating. I sensed a deep change in myself, then a touch of anxiety. How would I explain my reversal to Chuck and my six women friends? It would be like Benedict Arnold trying to rejoin the Colonists. I felt terribly guilty. I had spoken negatively about the baptism in the Holy Spirit and these "tongues speakers". As a Christian, I had a deep responsibility to right my wrongs.

Chuck was a reasonable fellow, open to new information and, best of all, accessible, but what about my women friends? If I could only get them to go with me to hear Pastor Bredesen and Dr. Reed! But how could that be managed on Friday night, the busiest night of the week?

It wasn't easy to make myself phone my friends, but I did, explaining what had happened. Margaret was first on my list. After a short prayer, I called. She was firm.

"Charla, you know I always play bridge on Friday night, I can't go. They can't play without me."

"Margaret, listen," I pleaded. "If you never do another thing for me, just go with me this evening and hear these speakers."

Finally she agreed. Five prayers and phone calls later, the other five consented to go. All six received the baptism in the Holy Spirit that evening.

Our excitement and joy in the Lord bubbled over all the way to North Hollywood, where my six friends insisted on coming into our house to continue talking about the things we had just learned.

"Are you going to tell Chuck what happened?" Margaret asked musically, as we entered the living room.

"Not right now," I replied. I had hoped to have a

quiet time alone with Chuck to share the experience.

Chuck knew something dramatic had taken place, I was sure, because snatches of our elated conversation had carried to the den where he was resting from a hard day's work.

After my friends left, he came immediately into the kitchen.

"Well, what happened to you?"

I explained that we had gone to a Christian retreat and my friends and I had been baptized in the Holy Spirit. He gave me a blank look.

"That's outside my range of experience." And it was, because in many churches, the Holy Spirit seems to be a forgotten member of the Trinity. "It's been a long day for both of us," he said. "Let's talk more about it in the morning."

After I checked the diaper of the blissfully sleeping Charles Curtis, we went to bed silently.

Over morning coffee, Chuck eagerly asked for more details. Paging through the Scriptures in my worn, black-leather Bible, I read verses concerning the baptism in the Holy Spirit, particularly Luke 11:13 — "If ye then, being evil, know how to give good gifts unto your children, how much more shall your heavenly Father give the Holy Spirit to them that ask Him."

Chuck set down his cup of coffee. His eyes were intense. "I want the Holy Spirit," he told me. "How can I receive Him? Can you pray for me?"

"I'm not sure, Chuck," I replied just as earnestly. "I think this has to be a special gift."

Months went by and Chuck kept praying that God would baptize him in the Holy Spirit, but no prayer language came to him. Being new to all this, I felt helpless.

Finally we heard about a conference in Visalia,

California where many had been baptized in the Holy Spirit. Chuck went with a friend. Both hungered for this blessing and when the speaker, Dennis Bennett, laid hands on these Lutheran brothers, they were filled to overflowing with the Spirit. A beautiful new language came from their mouths, and they drove all the way back home praising and worshipping God.

Chuck and I grew closer than ever. Both of us spoke freely of Jesus and shared experiences in our Christian growth. In the years before my baptism in the Holy Spirit, I could not speak the name "Jesus" in circles where this was not common. I would refer to "God" and in time, "Our heavenly Father," then, finally, to "Christ". After the baptism in the Holy Spirit, I could talk about Jesus even to casual acquaintances or strangers.

My life changed rapidly and markedly as it had many years before when I had received Christ as Lord and Saviour and was born again. How I treasured that memory!

As if it were yesterday, I remembered life in Michigan and my mother and grandmother, devout Christians who knew the love of God. My father, a practicing Roman Catholic, had not been able to find the power in his religion to deliver him from long-standing alcoholism. My mother had prayed long and ardently for his deliverance. When we had least expected it, my father, one of the early members of Alcoholics Anonymous, quit drinking and, soon afterwards, was converted to Christ at a Salvation Army meeting in Detroit.

During my earliest years in Michigan, I had attended a Methodist Sunday School with my mother and found it a dreary experience — the dark church basement near the dusty coal bin, the rickety folding chairs which often collapsed (I carry a scar above my right eye to this day from a fall there!) and the uninspired teaching that turned my view of the beautiful, colorful and exciting Bible into boredom. A girl who loved life and adventure, I counted the minutes which dragged by like ants walking through honey.

We moved to Richmond, California, in 1945, where my dad worked in the shipyards of nearby Vallejo until the end of World War II. Things changed quickly. Walking home on a Sunday evening, I became chilled through by the damp, knifing wind off San Francisco Bay. As I passed a brightly-lit little Southern Baptist church I thought, *"I will just step inside, get warm and then hurry home."* I expected to find a cozy vestibule; instead, I entered the back part of the sanctuary and, before I could retreat, a man handed me a hymn book and ushered me to a seat. I began to worry. My mother had expected me home by seven. I seemed to have a special knack for getting into strange predicaments.

These thoughts came to an abrupt end when the young minister, looking directly at me, said, "Christianity is not trying to keep an ever-changing list of do's and don'ts. It is a dynamic, life-changing encounter with Jesus Christ."

The warmth of that church both in temperature and spirit thawed me out, and I had a feeling of being safe, secure and loved by God as never before.

"Jesus offers you many things — a new life, among others," continued the minister. "Imagine that! He can make you free from guilt and fear — no matter what sin you have committed. God loves you. He wants you to accept His Son Jesus as Lord and Saviour. He wants to guarantee you a place in Heaven. All you have to do is turn away from your sin, invite Jesus into your heart and give Him control of your life. He wants to make you brand new — born again!"

I had come into this church for warmth but I had found far more. *How could anyone turn down an offer like that?*

And, suddenly, there I was at the altar. I received Jesus Christ and my heart seemed to fly and sing. More than anything else, I wanted to do things His way. Jesus had taken me in out of the cold. I was baptized on the next Sunday.

We moved to Van Nuys, Southern California, in 1946, where I sampled a series of different denominational churches, searching for years for a church like the little one in which I had met Jesus.

When I was sixteen, a girlfriend invited me to Emmanuel Lutheran Church in North Hollywood to hear a young evangelical pastor, Norman Hammer, who had extraordinary appeal to young people. Through his spiritual influence many were introduced to Christ and a great number entered full-time ministry.

On my first visit, I met one of Pastor Hammer's converts, Charles Pereau, a tall, slender, dark-haired, nineteen-year-old with luminous blue eyes and a winsome, shy smile.

Something deep inside me stirred. There was a special quality about Charles Pereau that I had never found in any other man — a deep compassion for others. We were drawn together by more than just the allure of the opposite sex. Both of us had an encounter with Jesus and we knew that God had special direction for our lives. Only a few months later, we traveled to Seattle, Washington to attend Bible school together and nine months later we became Mr. and Mrs. Charles Pereau.

Now as I reviewed how far Jesus had led Chuck

and me — to the baptism in the Holy Spirit — my thoughts raced back to summer camp, where we had prayed for a new spiritual dimension. How generously the Lord had answered that prayer!

I found myself now on a higher plateau, nearer to Jesus. I became painfully aware of sins in my life. A new boldness took away my reluctance to witness. Scriptures whose meanings were cloudy became clear. I was now a better communicator, a more confident Bible teacher.

Ministering with the power of the Holy Spirit is far more effective than ministering without. It is like mixing a cake with an electric mixer, rather than a wooden spoon.

Why had I resisted so strenuously? Does a loving Father give useless gifts to His children? Some persons say that tongues is the least of the gifts. No gift of God is unimportant. If it were so, Paul would not have said, "I would that ye all spoke with tongues . . ." (1 Corinthians 14:51).

Tongues is a pure and sweet communication, praise and adoration and thanks to the Lord. For the first time in my life, I loved myself and could, therefore, love God and my neighbor. My concern for humanity increased.

One of the most beautiful rewards from praying in tongues at will was the confidence I gained from His continual presence and the assurance that He is always giving me strength.

Over and above our spiritual gains, Chuck and I were delighted with events at home which helped kindle a desire in our children to be baptized in the Holy Spirit.

The friends with whom I had gone to the Christian retreat began to meet in our home every Friday night to study the Scriptures, to learn more about our new spiritual dimension. Dana, Craig and Andrea often heard us talk with excitement about the joy in living in the Spirit and they, too, asked Jesus for the baptism in the Holy Spirit. Almost overnight the boys were blessed with it, and were given a prayer language — but not Andrea.

Now fourteen, Andrea had lived in a semi-silent world since her early childhood, due to chronic ear infection and damage to her hearing apparatus. An outpatient of the John Tracy Clinic in Los Angeles, she had a seventy percent hearing impairment in one ear and thirty percent in the other. There was calcification in her inner ears and thick scar tissue on her ear drums. Her ailments were not correctable by surgery.

One Sunday night when Chuck and I attended our church's monthly service of intercession, we were surprised to see Andrea there. She came up and knelt at the altar for prayer.

Pastor Wold bent toward her and asked a question. Andrea, who reads lips expertly, answered.

"What do you suppose she is telling him?" I inquired of Chuck.

That night at home, I asked her.

"I told the pastor that because of my hearing problem I'm doing miserably in my schoolwork and I'm an emotional mess about it. I asked him to pray for God to help me. He did, and something strange happened while I was walking home."

"What was that?"

"God gave me a new language," she said.

I was overjoyed, even though that was not the response Andrea had prayed for. Yet I was slowly beginning to learn that maybe God knew more about handling His business than I did.

One evening Andrea said something rather

peculiar.

"They shouldn't let so many cars and trucks use our street!"

"Well, Andrea, it's a public street. There's nothing we can do about it," I replied.

While she was studying on another occasion, she asked, "Why do you have to have the TV on so loud?"

On still another evening, she asked, "What is that 'er' sound?"

It took us all a while to figure out what she was talking about. "That's the refrigerator," Chuck replied.

"Does it always make that noise?"

"Why, yes."

And still we didn't realize what was happening until I received a phone call from the Walter Reed Jr. High School, where Andrea had recently enrolled.

A nurse informed me that Andrea had had her ears tested by the North Hollywood Health Department.

"Her hearing is now perfectly normal." she said.

Praise the Lord! God has given us a miracle.

We had missed many signals that Andrea was coming out of her semi-silent world into the world of distracting noises.

God had corrected the cause of her poor schoolwork and emotional problems.

Praise and thanksgiving filled our home and, like all of us, Charles Curtis thrived in this atmosphere.

Perhaps because of the difference in his appearance from other family members and the fact that an adopted child is special, Charles Curtis was showered with attention and love; although Craig, being the youngest, at first found it a little hard to share attention with his baby brother.

One night when the children and Chuck had settled down, I stole a last look at Charles Curtis, asleep in his crib, the hint of a smile on his sweet face. *"He IS beautiful,"* I told myself and broke into prayer.

"Oh, thank you, Lord, for this priceless gift. God bless him and use him to further Your Kingdom."

Suddenly I felt overwhelmed with God's love. I felt privileged.

How vigorously I had resisted the blessing of Charles Curtis, just as I had the baptism in the Holy Spirit. I overflowed with thanks. God had given us more than a new life to help to grow toward Him. He had given us another son.

I would have been even more thankful if I had known then that our relationship with Charles Curtis was to revolutionize our way of life — particularly mine. Soon I would be vaulted into the greatest adventure in faith and love that any person could possibly experience.

But first, there was earthly work to do. We would have to start the adoption procedure so that Charles Curtis could become Charles Curtis Pereau.

I hoped we could breeze right through but suspected we would come smack up against roadblocks. Even friends who wished us the best said that the bureaucracy and the letter of the law would make adoption a roaring headache to us.

They proved to be right.

5

ADOPTION? IMPOSSIBLE!

Our attorney had started adoption proceedings with the County of Los Angeles and headed Chuck, Charles Curtis and me to the Department of Social Service and our first roadblock — a social worker who knew the regulations down to every "whereby", "wherefore" and semi-colon.

That morning we asked God to grant us favor with those in authority, praying for His wisdom and grace in presenting our case, because the State of California then was not kindly disposed toward independent and interracial adoptions. We were ten years too early.

She hunched down, round-shouldered, over our papers, shaking her head and clucking ominously. Finally, she pushed them aside.

"These are not legal," she said. "The infant's mother did not speak Spanish, and your interpreter did not have a full knowledge of Zapotec."

I was too stunned to reply.

She noted this reaction and said, "I'm sorry," in the least sorrowful voice I have ever heard.

I was upset but kept my feelings in check.

Chuck's usually smiling and agreeable face was like the black clouds of a thunderstorm, ready to break loose with thunder and lightning.

I prayed, and at least a degree of composure settled over us.

"What would happen if we gave up this child?" I asked, dreading what she might say and remembering my solemn promise to his mother. "He would be placed in a foster home, " responded the social worker. "You see, he's not legally adoptable." It seemed to me she didn't show human consideration for Charles Curtis, his future or our feelings.

"Do you know what would happen if we followed that route?" I asked. She arranged papers and forms in a neat pile. "You place him in a foster home, and he'll be a financial burden and responsibility to taxpapers of the State of California."

I studied her face for a sign of response. Apparently she had already made up her mind but I went on anyway, "He'll continue from home to home. Finally, he won't be suitable for a home. Then he'll go to an institution, Juvenile Hall and finally, to prison."

Chuck nodded vigorously, saying, "We are willing to take this child as our own, give him a home — not at the taxpayers' expense but our own and raise him as our son."

The great stone faces of Mount Rushmore would have shown more human compassion.

"Do you have an Indian family who would adopt Charles Curtis?" I asked.

"No."

"We could keep him until you find one." She didn't disagree, so I continued. "If you could only locate an Indian family which would give him love, security and a good home, I would give him up."

"I wouldn't," Chuck spat.

"As I said before, Mr. and Mrs. Pereau, you have no legal right . . . ".

Chuck raised his voice. "Well, just *try* to get him away from us!"

"Chuck!" I interrupted. If he continued so antagonistically, the social worker would never let us keep Charles Curtis. Chuck picked up my brain waves and calmed down.

Suddenly the social worker asked, "What do you do culturally as a family?"

That one stopped me. I tried to direct my thoughts down the cultural lines pursued by the Pereau family. It's pretty hard to answer a question like, "What do you do culturally," with a squirming baby in your arms. I felt the pressure of being on the defensive, groping for the right reply, asking myself what most parents with four children do culturally or socially.

Chuck came up with an answer: "We're very active in our church, Charla is a Camp Fire Girls' leader and helps with Cub Scouts. We camp and hike."

It was impossible to detect whether or not Chuck's reply satisfied her and, at long last, the two-hour ordeal was over.

The case worker looked up from her desk, appraised us for what seemed minutes, then said, "I'm going to come to your home for a visit."

The cause didn't seem entirely lost.

As promised — or threatened — she did. She measured room dimensions, far more interested in physical "air-space" than in the loving acceptance of Charles Curtis by our family. Nobody had to tell me the kind of written report she would put together about us and the environment in which Charles Curtis was living.

But even at that, I prayed that something good would result from her inspection. I knew that our attorney would receive a copy of the report and read it to me.

When he called, a few weeks later, his voice was dead.

"Charla, I hate to tell you this, but the report was negative."

Her reflection on our ability to provide the proper physical, cultural, intellectual and social environment for Charles Curtis didn't bother me as much as the fact that a judge's final decision on the adoption would be based mainly on that report.

"So that's the end of the line?" I asked, fearing his answer.

"No, Charla, just the beginning."

I could have jumped for joy.

"We'll take the matter to the Burbank court. A judge over there just granted a baby to Jimmy 'Schnozzle' Durante, who's in his 70's. Let's wait until we can get on his calendar."

We did. Although the case worker's weighty report was against us, we did appear to have a judge sympathetic to independent adoptions and human considerations. Not only would we and Charles Curtis appear, but also Dana, eight, and Craig, seven, and our daughter who was thirteen. I wasn't concerned about Andrea, but the boys — who knows what chance remark they would make that would explode our presentation? Then just two days before the hearing Dana broke his arm, a complication which he and we could have done without.

Chuck and I prayed, as we always do about major events in our lives. Usually, I can then drop my concerns, but somehow, I couldn't on that morning as the whole Pereau gang — Charles Curtis in my arms — assembled in the judge's chambers.

A man in his late fifties, greying at the temples, the judge appeared rather substantial in his bulky, black robe. From behind his desk, he swept a quick glance over us as we sat before him in a row of straight-backed chairs. Attorney Rhinehart introduced us to him individually. His face showed a trace of a smile at each introduction and I began to feel better. His eyes kept coming back to Dana and his arm in a white cast and sling.

"Oh, no, he's going to start with the boys," I told myself, and he did.

"Dana," he said. "How did you break your arm?"

Dana, grey-blue eyes sparkling, stood up, tall and slender — a junior-size Chuck (an ego the size of a refrigerator).

"A silly accident, your Honor. I fell off my bike."

The judge smiled. "Come over here, Dana." Dana quickly walked behind the desk of the judge, who extended his right arm. "Feel right here, Dana."

Dana felt the judge's arm.

"I had a break in my arm when I was about your age."

The judge picked up a ball point pen on his desk.

"Reach that broken arm over, Dana," he ordered. Dana did, and the judge scribbled his autograph on the cast.

Then he addressed Craig. "What do you think of this baby?" he asked. Craig self-consciously rose from his chair, broad, square with beautiful posture, the lights glinting off his brown hair — a sensitive, shy look in his brown eyes.

In a few stumbling but sincere words, Craig wrapped it up: "He's . . . he's my brother, Your Honor."

If Dana and Craig had been anointed in heaven they couldn't have conducted themselves better.

The judge asked them to sit down, directed routine questions to Andrea, Chuck and me, and turned his attention to the social worker's report. His fixed expression didn't change an iota as he read. Then he looked at us all, stopping for an instant on Charles Curtis. A sunburst of a smile broke out on his face.

"Some of these social workers can't see beyond the ends of their noses," he announced. "Adoption granted."

A cheer went up from the Pereaus. David had again overcome Goliath!

6

GOD DELIGHTS IN USING THE INSIGNIFICANT

A shudder went through me after I read the letter.

"It could have happened to Charles Curtis," I told myself.

The letter from Pastor William Nehrenz of the mission in Oaxaca had arrived on our son's first birthday. It was like a frigid wind:

"Shortly after your fellow was born there was a famine in the land and a plague of diptheria struck the Zapotec Indian tribe. More than one hundred babies died in our parish alone."

"The boy's mother and I send love and appreciation to you for taking him away from here. We thank God . . .".

I thanked God, too.

I wondered, *"Why did the God of the universe take one little Indian boy out of danger and move him 3,000 miles away to safety and security in North Hollywood?"*

My most persistent theory was that Charles Curtis had been preserved to grow up to be a missionary and return to his people. When he was two and a half years old, he brought home a Sunday school paper showing a small boy skipping, a mongrel dog and a huge sun in the sky. The headline on the page was, "Look What God Has Done For Me." I felt this was a prophecy.

I looked from the headline to this beautiful, happy child and again thought of God's amazing grace in picking him up and moving him all those miles to us. That Sunday morning I rededicated him and myself to the Lord and again asked myself why an Indian boy had been spared.

At least a part of the answer came to me several years later — although I didn't immediately recognize it. A *Newsweek* shocked me into a new awareness of an acute and growing social problem south of the border. A staff correspondent, Bruce van Voorst, wrote about a "vast army of abandoned children":

"Latin America's major cities are swarming with well over a million children whose families are unable or unwilling to take care of them."

It told of barefoot kids (some as young as five) swarming in bands, ragged, dirty, lice-infested and diseased, pawing through garbage cans or stealing food from peddler's carts. The children wandered among human derelicts and drunken men and women. Flies crawled on them, they slept under bridges, on trash heaps, in cemeteries and sewers. Very young teenage girls were thrust or sold into prostitution for survival. Small boys were becoming panhandlers, thieves, pimps or dope pushers.

A wave of nausea came over me. More than a million children like Charles Curtis were existing in and being corrupted by this Sodom and Gomorrah. *"Lord,"* I cried out, *"If only I could do something to help."*

Then the past smacked me down. How could someone as insignificant as myself make even a tiny dent in a problem so tremendous? I had no illusions about myself. I had been a failure as a daughter, wife, mother, woman and Christian.

I had broken my parent's heart by eloping with Chuck at sixteen, throwing away a four-year university scholarship. In my early years of marriage I had been unloving, self-centered and an inflexible nag, causing a six months separation and almost a divorce.

As a mother, I had false pride that kept me bound to a rigid schedule. A spotless house was more important than listening and reading to the children and playing with them.

I had been a failure as a woman, comparing myself unfavorably with other women in appearance and abilities.

I was a failure as a Christian, reading and talking about love but not practicing it. I could not pray out loud until after my baptism in the Holy Spirit.

On my own, I could do nothing about the abandoned children, but, with God, maybe I could. References from the Bible unreeled before me. God delights in using those with faults — the insignificant and the failures.

". . . Not many wise men after the flesh, not many mighty, not many noble are called."

There is evidence of this from Genesis to Revelation: Noah, a drunkard; Moses, a murderer; David, an adulterer; Rahab, a prostitute; Mary, the Lord's mother, an ordinary peasant girl; Matthew, an avaricious materialist; John and James, the vengeful sons of Thunder, and Peter, a coward who denied the Lord.

Even Jesus Christ's life was a failure from every

standpoint but God's. Neither joy nor sorrow deterred Him from His purpose: to die for our sins and redeem those who choose to be redeemed by His blood.

God delights in using the insignificant and He can even use our failures. He delights in using those totally dependent upon His grace and supply.

I had no idea that He was beginning to use me. Then, in 1965, while I was Superintendent of the Vacation Bible School at Emmanuel Lutheran Church, I worked on a mission project to gather clothing, blankets and other supplies for a Tijuana orphanage being helped by California Lutheran Bible School.

Because Chuck had a truck and a willing heart, we volunteered to haul these things. We had never visited Mexico, so it sounded exciting. With our truck almost brimming over, we headed south to Tijuana and the Rosepark Orphanage, overlooking a garbage dump. When we unloaded there, all I could see was children with little brown faces — so many of them similar in appearance to my boy at home. This was a real live demonstration of the *Newsweek* article, every word of which was etched on my brain. Since then I have never been able to shut my eyes to Mexico and its homeless children.

That was the first of many trips to orphanages in cities near the United States: Tijuana, Ensenada and Mexicali. There were different orphanages but they were the same in many respects — inefficiently organized and administered, usually overstocked with supplies — mountains of clothing, a hopeless mixture of pants, shirts, jackets, socks, underwear and mismatched shoes, piles of unsorted canned and packaged foods and doctor's medical and vitamin samples that nobody could read, categorize or put to use.

This lack of organization extended to the upbringing of the children. In most instances the orphanages offered only clothing, food and shelter from the elements. With no vocational training, the children were not prepared to make a living when turned out on the street at the age of 14.

All the orphanages really taught was dependency and that the world owes them a living. Their hands were out to receive American charity. Worst of all, the children had no training in the Bible or Christian living. Their social patterns warped them for the rest of their lives. Their future was a ragged, hazardous existence on the streets of Tijuana, Ensenada and Mexicali; a hodge-podge of the worst of two cultures — certainly not the true Mexico.

I cried out to God, *"There must be a better way to supply the needs of these children."*

Then, in the summer of 1966, I became enchanted by a feature article about the remote village of Baja, California — Colonia Vicente Guerrero. I began my prayers for the village, never dreaming that these prayers would eventually send Chuck and me there and involve us in an adventure of faith and love for the rest of our lives.

MEXICO
280 DISTANCE BETWEEN CITIES IN KILOMETERS
(3:52) DRIVING TIME
PACIFIC OCEAN
Gulf of Mexico
Gulf of California
Gulf of Tehuantepec
SIERRA MADRE OCCIDENTAL
SIERRA MADRE ORIENTAL
SIERRA MADRE DEL SUR
INTERAMERICAN HIGHWAY
Yucatan Peninsula
Arizona
EL SALVADOR
Tijuana
Ensenada
COLONIA GUERRERO
San Quintin
San Felipe
Puerto Peñasco
Sonoita
Nogales
Hermosillo
Bahia Kino
Ciudad Obregón
Yaqui R.
Janos
Ciudad Juarez
Chihuahua
Conchos
Santo Domingo
La Paz
San José del Cabo
Culiacán
Mazatlán
Durango
Torreón
Saltillo
Monterrey
Monclova
Nuevo Laredo
Mier
Reynosa
Brownsville
Matamoros
Orleans
Ciudad Victoria
Soto La Marina
Mante
Tampico
Zacatecas
Huizache
Valles
Aguascalientes
San Luis Potosi
Tepic
Guadalajara
Lake Chapala
Puerto
Manzanillo
Salamanca
Queretaro
Pachuca
Tuxpan
Morelia
MEXICO
Toluca
Puebla
Veracruz
Orizaba
Iguala
Taxco
Altamirano
Zihuatanejo
Playa Azul
Huajuapan de Leon
OAXACA
Acapulco
Tinotepa Nal.
Acayucan
Villahermosa
Tuxtla Gutierrez
Tehuantepec
Tapachula
Usumacinta
Campeche
Mérida
Puerto Juarez
Cozumel
Felipe Carillo Puerto
Chetumal
Francisco Escárcega
Belize
193 (3:14)
196 (2:42)
190 (3:45)
266 (3:43)
422
(6:25)
161 (2:58)
279 (4:19)
256
(3:36)
375 (5:07)
260 (3:46)
431
692 (9:25)
457 (6:22)
249 (3:49)
230
280
(6:12)
253 (3:52)
(5:44)
342
(5:05)
287 (4:33)
309 (4:17)
224 (3:35)
(17:00)
290 (4:29)
370
(2:02)
136
318 (6:06)
293 (4:38)
130
108
(1:35)
(3:07)
190
167 (259)
227 (3:46)
318
216
204
(2:57)
383
(7:31)
213
(2:30)
348 (5:10)
361
(5:47)
248 (4:37)
64
127
(2:10)
186
349 (5:55)
360 (548)
339 (6:51)
339
215
(3:58)
183
(3:00)
192
(3:54)
233 (4:39)
252 (5:22)
221
(3:30)
228 (3:17)
248 (3:54)
290 (4:58)
481 (7:41)
255 (5:06)
297 (4:20)
381 (8:30)
147
(2:08)
250 (3:41)
322 (4:25)
273
(4:25)

7

STRANGE HAPPENINGS BELOW THE BORDER

It had been a long and eventful journey from the Lutheran Family Bible Camp in the pine-scented San Bernardino mountains to our adventures enroute to the remote Mexican village of Colonia Vicente Guerrero. Now, as we neared the Mexican border with Pedro, my confidence about bringing this orphan into the United States waned.

Then I laughed at myself. All of this doubt was weakening my faith. Hadn't I learned many times that Satan and his agents always use such darts of doubt to infect and then disease faith?

No matter how I prayed, the darts of doubt still kept coming at me. Just what were we going to say when the U.S. immigration officer asked about Pedro?

The whole truth of the matter would sound like fiction. "Well, you see, officer, we were in this little church in Guerrero, and this boy began foretelling his future with inspiration of the Holy Spirit by quoting Isaiah . . ." I could already see the expression on his face and hear a suppressed question, "What looney bin did you come out of?"

Chuck pulled the car to the side of the road.

"We've got problems about Pedro," he said simply. "But we have to remember that God, who led us into this situation, has no problems about Pedro at all. Let' s pray."

And we all prayed, silently and then out loud in the Spirit. Roy finished with "Our dear sister Charla acted out of love for You and this boy, Lord. She believes You want her to take Pedro home. This predicament is too much for our human hands, Lord. We're putting it into Your hands. You tell us that when we're delivered unto our enemy, You will fill our mouths with the right words to say. And God, we need the right words. We're counting on Your fulfillment of that promise now. Thank you, Lord. Amen!"

All of us, including Pedro echoed with fervent "Amens." Now, with confidence, we headed for the border — all eager to see how the Lord would handle our dilemma.

We braked to a stop and a sun-tanned immigration officier came to Chuck's window and looked into the car, first in the back seat at Roy and Neil.

"Nationality?"

"American" they replied.

"Where do you live?"

"North Hollywood."

Then he asked Chuck and me the same questions.

"American and North Hollywood," we responded.

We held our breath. Pedro was next. He looked at the boy, said nothing and waved us across. We were puzzled. Why didn't he ask the nationality of the boy who was obviously Mexican? How could he have missed seeing Pedro? What had God done to make our border crossing possible?

Upon our arrival home, the anxiety of the children and the couple baby-sitting them turned into excitement. As soon as we explained our tardiness, the children wanted to know all about Pedro, who smiled shyly at them. Well-meaning friends, eager to hear about the trip, came over. When we told our story of finding Pedro and what seemed to us a miraculous border-crossing, they appreciated our enthusiasm for God's answer to our prayer but accented the realities of the situation.

We could pay a sizeable penalty for taking an illegal alien over the border. One of our Job's comforters told us, "There's a $10,000 fine for that act!"

Now I was really upset. We knew nothing about legal procedure for bringing a Mexican national into the United States, but we would have to learn. Next day, via the phone, I found out that the basic document was a birth certificate.

I couldn't rest until I could find Pedro's parents, a copy of his birth certificate, and get him the appropriate papers to make him legitimate in the U.S. And again, the Lord worked miracles. Following bits and scraps of evidence, Pedro and I made eleven trips across the border to track down couples who might have been his parents and each time I failed. Each time he was sitting in plain sight of immigration officers but was never questioned. The shield of the Lord continued to protect his presence in the United States. A happy and warm person, Pedro was an instant hit with the family.

On the afternoon of one of our weekly evening prayer meetings, we learned that Jerry and Emma Jo Krause, friends from Costa Mesa, were driving over that night with Dave and Audrey Taylor. They wanted to tell us the details about God's leading them to move to Fort Worth, Texas. I felt a pang of regret, because Chuck and I were close to them and would miss their company, but, at the same time, I realized that they always were trying to align their lives to God's will.

Pedro, who by now could get by with his English, was in the den as usual for the prayer meeting. As Emma Jo talked, he listened attentively. Emma Jo kept looking at the boy as she spoke, but I thought little of it then. After the prayer meeting, I could no longer hold back my curiosity about their leaving to move to Texas.

"What sort of guidance did you get, Emma Jo?"

"The still small voice to both Jerry and me, a vision, and also a prophecy from Mother Bird, a lady in Huntington Beach baptized in the Holy Spirit and blessed with the gift of prophecy."

"Well, what specifically, was the vision?"

"Mother Bird saw us moving to Fort Worth, Texas and buying a factory there," responded Emma Jo. "Specifically, she saw a green freeway sign with the name of Fort Worth in white lettering and then, on the right side of the freeway, a church with a beautiful, close-cropped, green lawn on four sides, bordering the parking lot of a supermarket. The church had a 'For Sale' sign on it."

"How does the church tie in?"

"Charla, we don't know that yet. We'll find out when we get there."

It was getting late, so we said goodbye.

At about three o'clock in the morning the phone in our bedroom rang. I fumbled for it, noted the outrageous hour on the illuminated clock radio, and thought, *"Who in the world would pick such an unearthly time to call?"*

"Charla, this is Emma Jo."

"Is something wrong?" I asked in alarm.

"No, but I felt compelled to phone you. That boy who was in your den last night — Pedro . . . Well, let me start from the beginning. On the drive home, Jerry and I and Dave and Audrey talked about Pedro. Jerry and I got the strong feeling that we were supposed to offer him a home and education and take him to Texas."

I was surprised and troubled. Pedro and I had learned to communicate quite well, and Chuck and I already loved him like a son. The children thought he was the greatest and included him in their activities. How could we possibly part with Pedro?

"Oh, no!" I replied. "I'm sure that's not the Lord's timing, Emma Jo."

"Well, Dave and Audrey had the same strong feelings."

The conversation was too upsetting for me to continue — especially at three in the morning, so I made it brief.

"Why don't we talk about it tomorrow, Emma Jo? I've got to get some sleep. Good night."

Actually, it *had* been a good night until she had phoned. As for sleep, I did more tossing than sleeping.

Somewhere around seven a.m. when I was drinking my first cup of coffee, I was surprised by a phone call from Bea Barnett, a lovely Episcopalian lady in Woodland Hills.

Bea Barnett! How often from out of the blue I had heard from her in times of crisis! How often she had brought me a solution without having been told my problem!

"Charla, this is your old friend Bea. God brought you to mind this morning. Shall we pray?"

When Bea prayed in the Spirit, she was given divine insights, interpretations, exhortations and prophecies. We joined in this kind of prayer, and

Bea, who knew nothing about my differences with Emma Jo over Pedro said —

"God has used you and Chuck to salvage this boy's life from destruction, and he is calling on you now to be spiritually responsible, because he is giving another the responsibility for the boy's physical security and educational development. The boy will be leaving you."

I was seized with conviction that Emma Jo had been right. I had to give up what I couldn't give up. I phoned and told her, "Emma Jo, I had a witness from the Lord of the same thing that you had about Pedro. But we still have the problem of immigration papers."

Emma Jo asked if I would break the news to Pedro. I promised and hung up. With a leaden heart, I told him as gently as I could.

Tears began to form in his large, sensitive brown eyes. When I realized I might never see him again, they welled up in mine, too, and in an instant we were locked in a tight embrace, crying on each other's shoulders.

"But why must I go?" Pedro asked.

"It is the Lord's will."

"Why?" His brown eyes pleaded.

"I don't know exactly. The Lord does not always explain. But it is probably to help you fulfill your prophecy made in the little church in Guerrero." And I shared with him the first verse of the hymn, *Trust and Obey:*

"When we walk with the Lord
In the light of His word
What a glory he sheds on our way!
While we do His good-will, He abides
With us still
And with all who will trust and obey."

I dreaded the two-week interval until the day Chuck and I would have to give up Pedro. Soon it arrived and I had to take him to Jerry and Emma Jo. Pedro's possessions were all neatly packed in a small suitcase and Chuck called, "Pedro!"

No answer. He kept calling.

"Where is he?" I asked in anxiety, fearing that he might have run away. Chuck and I looked in every room, in the garage and then behind the garage, where we found him leaning against the stucco wall, head in his arms. He heard us and turned. He hadn't been crying, but his face was long.

"Chuck, don't send me away," he begged. "I work hard for you."

Chuck looked at Pedro, then at me and averted his face. Explanations had been fully made to Pedro. Chuck could add little more. "It is God's will for your life, Pedro. Sometimes we don't understand when God wants us to do something but everything works out right when we obey. You will see."

Pedro didn't see entirely, but shrugged his shoulders and accepted what had to be. Chuck put an arm around his shoulder and I followed as they walked to the back door together.

The Krauses took the boy to Texas and Emma Jo kept us posted by letter and phone calls. She was excited that Mother Bird's prophecy unfolded before their eyes in Texas: the big, green freeway sign with white letters, indicating Fort Worth and, on the right side of the freeway, a white church with vivid, close-cropped green lawn on all four sides, bordering the parking lot of a supermarket. What hit them all with impact was a "For Sale" sign hanging on the church.

Even Pedro, who had been reluctant to leave, was surprised at the accuracy of the picture and felt that, somehow, he was tied into this scene.

Why was this church so important in Mother Bird's prophecy? They did not know immediately. After getting settled in Fort Worth, they drove back to the area and noted that a "Sold" sign was now covering the "For Sale." Even then the answer was not plain. Out of curiosity, they again drove to the site a few months later and found that the church had been converted into a Christian high school.

Then they understood. Pedro was to enroll there. He did enroll and over the years, completed outstanding schoolwork. No natural parents could have been more proud of their son than were Jerry and Emma Jo. And Pedro thrived on their love and learned to love and trust them.

A strange event clouded the happiness of Jerry and Emma Jo when, two weeks before graduation, Pedro had a warning dream.

"I must leave for Mexico at once — alone," he declared.

"Oh, no, Pedro, you must go to school and take your final exams," insisted Emma Jo.

Pedro somberly shook his head.

"I must go to Mexico."

"Yes, of course, some day," Emma Jo assured him. "Some day you will graduate from seminary and you will minister to your people."

Pedro again shook his head.

"No, today. God told me I must go *today.*"

"Pedro, if you miss your final exams, you won't graduate. Graduation is the reward for your years of hard work. As soon as you have your diploma, we'll take you to Mexico," promised Emma Jo. Even as she spoke, Emma Jo realized she was not being totally fair to Pedro and his warning dream. Like Jerry and herself, he had the right to consider acting upon spiritual guidance. Yet such guidance should be confirmed by another witness or a scripture.

"Wait a minute, Pedro," Emma Jo said. "I'm going to phone Charla." Quickly she dialed my number, caught me at home in North Hollywood, explained the crisis and asked me to talk to Pedro.

"Pedro, it is of utmost importance that you do well on your finals for the glory of God and out of respect for the Krauses." Pedro was polite, as always, but he replied:

"I am sorry. I must leave for Mexico *now.*"

That was all he would say. Emma Jo came back on the phone and I advised:

"I don't pretend to understand all of this, but I've got a strong feeling that you're supposed to let Pedro go to Mexico — and right now!"

Emma Jo didn't understand fully either. She wanted to go with him but remembered that Pedro's dream had specified that he go alone. Hurriedly she gave Pedro money, drove him to the bus station, and put him on the first bus to Mexico.

That afternoon shortly after arriving home, she heard the doorbell ring. Opening up, she saw two immigration officers.

"We are looking for Pedro Praciato," one of them said.

"He isn't here," she replied.

"Well, can you tell us where he is?"

"Yes, he's in Mexico."

"Mexico?"

"Yes."

"Well, if he's in Mexico that ends it. Thank you very much."

And they left.

Next morning Pedro boarded a bus in Mexico and came back across the U.S. border in time to take his final exams and graduate with top honors from the

Christian high school.

Today Pedro is a minister of God, true to the prophecy which he uttered in the small church in Guerrero when we had first met him. He is preaching the gospel of the Lord to his people south of the border.

For a long period, he worked with Missionary David Booth, out of Guadalajara. Now, because of time, distance, and his complete dedication to his work, we have lost track of Pedro, but Jesus hasn't. So often God brings people with whom we share our lives; then, in His providence, they and we become separated from the human standpoint, but not in spirit.

8

A MIRACLE FOR CHRISTMAS, PLEASE!

Helpless!

That's how I felt standing near the altar.

Why on the spur of the moment had I insisted that someone lead a Christmas service for the people in the community? Usually on a Sunday or a holiday people met to pray, sing and testify.

It was our second Christmas in Guerrero and God had not yet raised up a pastor for the people. Our little church on the orphanage property was filled. Men, women and children had walked for many miles to meet together and worship the Lord. As the only one who felt the need for a service, I found myself responsible for the program and frightened for four reasons: I was an American, a woman in a man's culture, a person whose public speaking had been limited to Sunday School classes, and I couldn't hurdle the language barrier.

My vast Spanish vocabulary totalled three words, including "Adios," which I wished I could say to the congregation.

Chuck and I and our friends, Howard and Jean Wedell, had visited Baja for one purpose — to brighten Christmas for the eleven children and Juana with a roast turkey dinner and red and green-wrapped gifts with beautiful, big bows.

Juana, sensing my dilemma, rose from the expectant audience and joined me at the altar.

"I will translate for you."

"Great!" I said to myself. "Now all I need is something for you to translate."

Then a simple story by Ethel Barrett, of Gospel Light Publishing, which I had adapted for Sunday School use, came to mind. I told about a good shepherd, his flock of obedient sheep and a rebel sheep named Blister, who got into much trouble.

One night, he strayed from the flock, was chased far by a wolf and in panic, ran until his lungs ached. He fell off a precipice and lay broken in pain and crying on a ledge below. He cried so hard that he lost his voice and could only bleat in hopes that he would attract the attention of his shepherd.

The good shepherd, who hears the faintest bleat or cry, left his ninety-nine other sheep safe and secure, to look for the lost sheep. As he called out for the lamb, he heard his sorrowful bleat and climbed over the cliff. He tore his robe. Thorns cut his head and sharp rocks pierced his hands and feet, but he rescued the broken little lamb and carried him under his warm cloak to the flock and the fold.

"The Lord Jesus is this Good Shepherd." I told my listeners. "You are the lost sheep. Your Shepherd will hear your faintest cry. He is calling you by name this Christmas Day. Jesus will meet you and put you under His cloak and bring you safely to His Father. God will heal your diseases and anoint your eyes and ears with healing ointment. He is ready to heal and restore you and bring you to His Father's fold. Call upon the name of Jesus and be saved. If you would like me to pray for you, just come forward."

Forty individuals moved by the Holy Spirit came forward for prayer — many received Jesus as their personal Savior.

I was astonished, elated and then fearful. A woman with a black and brown, block-patterned shawl came forward with a dark-haired boy, a filthy adhesive-taped bandage over one eye. Speaking through Juana, she explained with gestures that much of that eye had been destroyed by an accidental shot from a .22 caliber rifle.

My heart went out to son and mother. Not too many years before, my nephew, lovingly called "Dickie-Bird," had gone on a camping expedition with his friend, Tim Matson, who had been shot in the eye with a BB gun and was hospitalized for weeks. *"What in the world was the condition of this boy's eye after being hit with a real shell?"* I asked myself. There probably wasn't much eye left!

As the mother continued speaking rapidly, I went through all sorts of mental gymnastics. *"Maybe I could take the boy to the States to a doctor."* And then a practical question dashed that idea to earth: *"Where in the world would I get the money to pay hospital and doctor bills for such delicate surgery?"*

Then came another idea. *"Where is the nearest medical help in Mexico?"* On the heels of that thought came still another. *"No doctor in the world can make an eye."*

I kept looking into the mother's earnest, brown face, as she reminded me, "The Señora said that Jesus Christ could heal." Her almost black eyes pleaded with childlike faith for me to produce a miracle in Jesus' name, believing that if I would only pray for that boy, he would be healed.

I began to squirm, but there was no getting away. The burden was on me and inwardly I cried for help:

"Dear God, I can't make an eye. You know, I can't make an eye."

Somewhere in my inner recesses came a firm response: *"But I can."* And, by faith, realizing that this mother had the gift of faith, I laid hands on that child's head and prayed out loud, "Dear God, I can't make an eye, but *You* can, and I claim a total restoration of sight to this little lamb of yours. May my hands be the healing hands of Jesus and make him every whit whole!"

Nothing seemed to happen so the mother and her son left for home. The next morning as we were packing the car to head back to the States, the mother and her son came to see us. My heart rocketed upward. The boy's bandage was off. There was not a mark on his face or eye!

I hadn't seen the eye under the bandage but later learned that two reliable witnesses had observed the damaged eye right after the accident.

Without a doubt, God had worked a creative miracle!

9

TROUBLE IN TWO PLACES

Often I have wished to be two persons so that, while working in Colonia Vicente Guerrero, I could also be running my home in North Hollywood, or while in North Hollywood, I could be handling problems in Guerrero.

Let me be specific. On a weekend in May, 1967, Chuck and I filled a small truck with supplies and foods needed at the orphanage. Our dear friends and neighbors, Ken and Bev Liskum, offered to take care of Charles Curtis, then six years old. I made Andrea the commanding officer of the older boys in the home fort.

So that Chuck could be back in time for work on Monday morning, we left after prayer group on a Friday night, driving the wearying, eye-straining, nerve-wracking route down the Baja Peninsula. We arrived in Guerrero in the morning darkness before sunup, blew out the kerosene lamp and plopped on one of the beds with our clothes on.

A few minutes after our eyelids closed, I felt a powerful urge to go back home. *This is ridiculous,* I told myself. *We just got here.* But I knew it wasn't.

These signals don't always come at our human convenience. They are intended to guide or warn us of some happening.

Chuck was already in a deep sleep and I hated to disturb him, but the signal grew stronger. Finally, I nudged him gently.

"I hate to say this, Chuck, but I believe we're supposed to go home.

He groaned and then muttered, "We just got here."

"I don't know why, but I can't get rid of this strong impression that we're supposed to go home."

Chuck stretched like a big cat and grudgingly admitted, "I think we should be obedient to those inner signals."

We struggled to our feet and, dragging with fatigue, managed to unload the truck, then drove all day, pulling into the Liskum's driveway at about six that evening. Ken and Bev met us at the door, surprised to see us so early.

"Thank God, you've come," said Ken. "Just this morning, Charles Curtis had an accident and broke his leg."

There he was in the living room on an end of a big couch, a full, white cast on one leg, looking small and lost.

I thanked God, for again He had answered our need before the problem had arisen. We had been on the road for several hours before Charles Curtis' accident had happened.

Immediately Ken had recognized that the leg was broken, but he was stopped because we had left no medical release so that he could get a doctor's treatment for our boy. Curtis was in pain and they were in a quandary when they got the idea of enlisting a Christian physician, Olaf Fisher.

It is not easy tracking down a medical doctor on a weekend, but they reached Dr. Fisher by phone. He rushed over to the Liskum's home, picked up Charles Curtis, took him to his office, X-rayed him, set the bone, put the leg in a cast, drove the boy back to the Liskum's and — the topping on the cake — refused payment.

After treatment by the doctor, Charles Curtis wasn't troubled so much by the pain as by the need to be with his parents in this emergency. And God knew and alerted us, as He does in many crises.

Never had I wished more for the ability to be in two places at one time than after my first head-on collision with poverty in Baja, California. Even in a completely different world of North Hollywood, California, it was impossible to crowd out of my mind the experience I had had near Ruben Jaramillo, a small village about 17 miles north of the orphanage. How I wanted to help!

I was driving Chuck's blue Chevy truck past Ruben Jaramillo when a woman flagged me down. She wore a man's ragged old cardigan sweater and carried an infant in a hammock type sling on her back. It took me a few seconds to understand what she had been doing before she saw me: kneeling next to the dirt road filling a baby bottle with muddy rain-water from a rut in the road to nurse her child.

Revulsion and pity surged through me at the same time. I jumped out of the car and walked over to her. She could see I was an American but spoke to me in the only language she knew, Spanish. I then understood only a small amount of Spanish. Nouns were no problem, but verbs were impossible. Desperate to communicate, she placed my hand on her forehead to show me that she had a high fever. Then she touched her breast, indicating that the "leche" (her milk) had dried up. She had nothing to feed the infant.

"Tiene leche?" she asked me. I almost broke into tears. I had no milk and shook my head to let her know. Obviously the child was sick, very sick. My first impulse was to offer her money to buy milk, but there wasn't a store around. All I had was packages of instant mashed potatoes. I gave her several and asked her to mix it with "agua pura" (clean water). It was hard to convey that I would drive to the orphanage 17 miles away (two and one-half hours by what they called a road) and return with milk early the next morning.

Before the sun rose, I was already enroute with a huge carton of powdered milk as well as canned milk, hoping that I wouldn't arrive too early for the Martinez family. I was too late. They were already behind the hut burying their dead baby.

I had never expected to see real hunger and starvation and life and death at their bare granite existence: skin-and-bones children with pot bellies and starving dogs with wash-board ribs and eyes almost bulging out of their heads.

That winter in Ruben Jaramillo — about 172 miles from the United States border — 37 people starved to death.

Rarely, since becoming a Christian, have I felt the least bit unhappy about our family's moderate financial circumstances. If I ever did, seeing conditions in Baja, California, would have changed all of that.

Such an experience is like speeding along on a plain of prosperity and suddenly plunging over a cliff into poverty. Many a time I have prayed for the souls and bodies of families living in the Ejidos, communities made up of land seized by the Mexican government and then divided into small parcels open for those who would settle there. Certain obligations came with the ground, as with homesteading. How these people who had never owned much of anything longed for a piece of land, something of their very own. And, with no briefing about the hostile environment, they swarmed to the area. Unable to cope, some died.

Most parts of the Baja Peninsula are barren, flat tableland. Unlike the United States pioneers and homesteaders, who lived many glorious pages of American history, these eager settlers found almost no water, wood and other materials for sustaining life and building shelter.

When they dug wells, water too salty to drink usually came up. A freshwater well was a rarity. Often the people had to walk a mile to fill buckets and then carry them back to their huts — water used sparingly for sanitation, cooking and drinking.

Building huts — about 10' x 10' — was not easy either. Not finding the materials they needed, they worked with what they had, hacking down the stock of agave cactus with machetes and setting pieces side by side in the ground, holding them in place with strong, fibrous weeds or cornstalks and plastering them with mud.

Similar treatment was given to roofs. Fortunate ones kept out the cold, heat and rain with roofs of tar paper. The not-so-fortunate used cardboard boxes, pieces of scrap metal, flattened tin cans and cactus. During the hard rains, these roofs leaked and floors puddled.

Grocery stores as we know them were then nonexistent. Families in fairly good financial shape had a few goats and chickens. Others lived on beans and corn and what they could get by trading them.

Many friends asked me pointed questions about

the poverty that took the life of the Martinez baby and 36 others in that unusually cold winter. How could God create more people than He could feed? Well, I don't believe a loving God would ever create more people than His earth can feed. It is my belief that, with starvation, the basic problems are not with God but with the indifference and greed among people.

That tragedy behind the little hovel in Ruben Jaramillo jolted me, shattering my values — material and spiritual — fitting them together in a new pattern. Never before have I been so painfully sensitive to food waste and to the need for good stewardship in the use of supplies and money that God gives me.

At one time, I thought that tithing was the whole answer: "Give 10 per cent to the church and, Charla, that's all there is to it." Now I know that's just the beginning. A truth struck me like lightning. Giving is not so much a matter of percentages but more than we can afford. If we are living at the same level of affluence as other people in a similar income bracket, we are giving too little. At least that's my yardstick for myself. It's not so much what external pressures impose upon you to give, but what God the Holy Spirit prompts you to give. We know little about sacrificial giving — that which costs us something.

After all, we're not giving what is ours. In almost every Lutheran church, a certain song is sung: "We give Thee but thine own. What ere the gift may be, all that we have is thine alone, a sacred trust for thee."

Adventures in giving are almost as great as in loving. Actually, they are interwoven. For instance, after a devastating earthquake in Guatelmala, a flyer from World Missionary Assistance told us we could provide a house for a homeless family for $300. Imagine, a whole house for that little!

So I said, "Let's see how much we can save from our food budget to buy a house for a homeless Guatemalan family." What did we do? We cut out the goodies that are so bad for you: cookies, cake, pie, whipping cream, potato chips, and crackers — those unnecessary evils.

We also cut on other nonessential expenditures. Instead of buying expensive cleaning products — as one example — we went back to basics, making our own low-cost cleaners from vinegar and ammonia. We began using terry towels instead of paper and handkerchiefs rather than Kleenex. We bought shampoo by the gallon at beauty supply stores. A Santa Monica thrift shop became our family boutique.

What a joyful time we had! In a little over eight weeks, we had the $300. And did my cup run over? It wasn't a sacrificial thing. It was a game. Then we gradually increased our giving until we were up to forty percent of our income.

Did we do without anything important on that 40 percent level? Not really. Remarkable things that God promises us in Malachi 3:10 began to happen without our asking anything from anybody.

One afternoon I came home and found the near empty freezer in our garage filled to capacity with packages of meat. Harry and Betty Sherda, wonderful friends who owned beef on the hoof, shared their abundance with us. Carl Calderhead, who owned a Union service station in Brentwood, picked up our car and installed new brakes. Many exciting things like that happened, and instead of having less, we seemed to have more.

Giving at a high level is both a delight and an

adventure, but I honestly recognize that everyone is not called to it. Those who don't give in joy shouldn't give. After all, the Lord loves a cheerful giver.

As sad as the infant's death was in the ejido of Ruben Jaramillo, it was not the end of everything there. Suddenly the cause of this ejido was my cause. On every trip to Guerrero I would bring a box of clothing and some food to my newly found friends.

Before too long, I realized that our family — and our prayer group — couldn't meet the tremendous needs of this village, mainly due to our method of distribution.

Often as we handed out clothing and other supplies from the back of a truck or station wagon, the aggressive and greedy individuals seized most of the things, while those with desperate needs often got nothing. I was upset and prayed for guidance. God gave me an idea. The greatest requirement of the people was items for new babies and their mothers.

I made Señora Martinez my source of information for any woman who was about to have a baby or who had just had one, and hand-carried an infant's layette with diapers and clothing to the family.

Many people in this area of Baja California were illiterate. When a Mexican family wanted to register a birth or to complete legal documents — they didn't make an "X" as in the United States — but in the office of the Delegado, the local magistrate, they would put their thumb on a stamp pad and press it on any document that needed a "signature."

When I wasn't free to go to Baja, Chuck went on his own — usually with a truckload of supplies for certain specific families of Ruben Jaramillo. Once during the glow of seeing the happiness that clothing, shoes and blankets bring, Chuck was jolted by

Señor Martinez, who looked up into his face, and asked a direct question:

"You and Señora Pereau are kind to bring us clothing and food, but when will you bring someone to tell us about God?"

Chuck had no ready answer. With help from Walt Henry, he had been scrambling to make the old orphanage livable, building a septic tank and connecting toilets and showers to it. He hadn't had the time to think about evangelizing the ejido. Upon his return to North Hollywood, Chuck told me what had happened.

"Charla, if I ever heard a Macedonian call, that was it." I thought carefully about his reference to the Apostle Paul's vision in Acts 16:9. Something had to be done to satisfy the hunger of these people to know the reality of God. That something, for the moment, was prayer to find an evangelist who could speak Spanish fluently.

The answer was not long in coming. At Thanksgiving time, a man named Marty Savedra, from San Clemente, came down to the orphanage with his wife, walked around the place, saw the children whom he thought were great, and then fell into deep thought.

"Isn't there someplace around here where I can go and hand out tracts?" he asked.

That lit a spark in me. *"Aha,"* I thought. *"Maybe I've got an evangelist here."* Turning toward him, I asked: "Marty, do you speak Spanish?"

"Do I speak Spanish?" He retorted. "Like a native."

"I know just where you should go," I said, telling him of Chuck's experience at Ruben Jaramillo. Marty, delighted with the opportunity, drove up the road with me to my friends, the Martinez'.

In my pidgeon-Spanish, I told them that Marty was there to explain to them the Good News of salvation in the name of Jesus. Señora Martinez' brown face beamed. In her layers of sweaters, she went out to bring back her neighbors. Within a matter of minutes, a crowd of people assembled in front of the cactus and mud-walled Martinez' hut.

Marty told the age-old story of the concept of God and His people and the sacrifice of His son for our sins. He told it simply and movingly in Spanish. Tears began to roll down cheeks, as the people kneeling down in the dust felt a true conviction of sin and repentance. There were genuine conversions and commitments to God, the source and supplier of all good things.

What a stunning experience. Much of the ejido — some 78 persons — came to know Jesus as Lord and Saviour. My heart abounds with joy to this day as I drive past Ruben Jaramillo and see, on the right side a number of houses with simple crosses on their roofs — symbolic of that Thanksgiving Day revival when they were born again.

Always filled with compassion for the poor, Marty came up with an enterprise which he thought would help make Ruben Jaramillo self-supporting in high protein food. He chose to set up the Martinez family as entrepreneurs in the egg business.

"Charla," he told me. "I'm going to get them cages and a couple dozen laying hens. Once the flock grows, they'll have eggs for the whole ejido."

I regretted having to dampen his enthusiasm. "Marty, your intentions are wonderful, but I'm afraid the plan won't work. I know conditions around here. Meat is a rarity. Before the flock will grow large enough to supply the ejido with eggs, the chickens will have been eaten."

Undaunted, Marty went through with his plan, but, unfortunately, it didn't work. As he commented to someone afterwards, "They ate the goose that laid the golden eggs."

Although Marty's project to satisfy physical hunger in Ruben Jaramillo failed, his effort to satisfy spiritual hunger succeeded admirably. With the spiritual nourishment came material changes. Today there are good roads past the ejido — not paved, true enough — but hardpacked dirt roads, two small churches, two tiny stores, several stucco houses and even a few homes with glass windows and some electrically lit places. Ruben Jaramillo is on its way to better living and greater spirituality.

Charla's Children

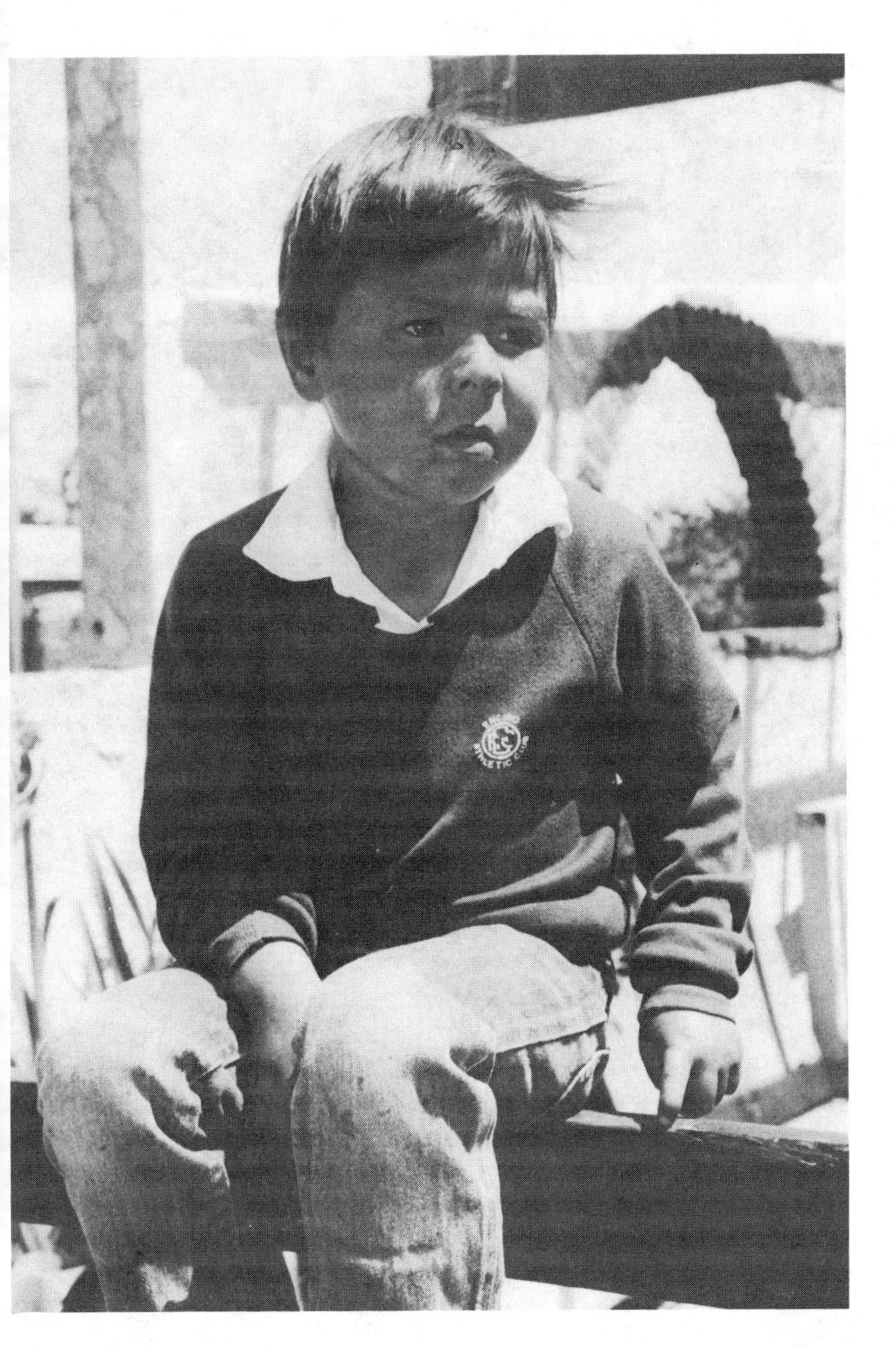

CESAR

LUIS

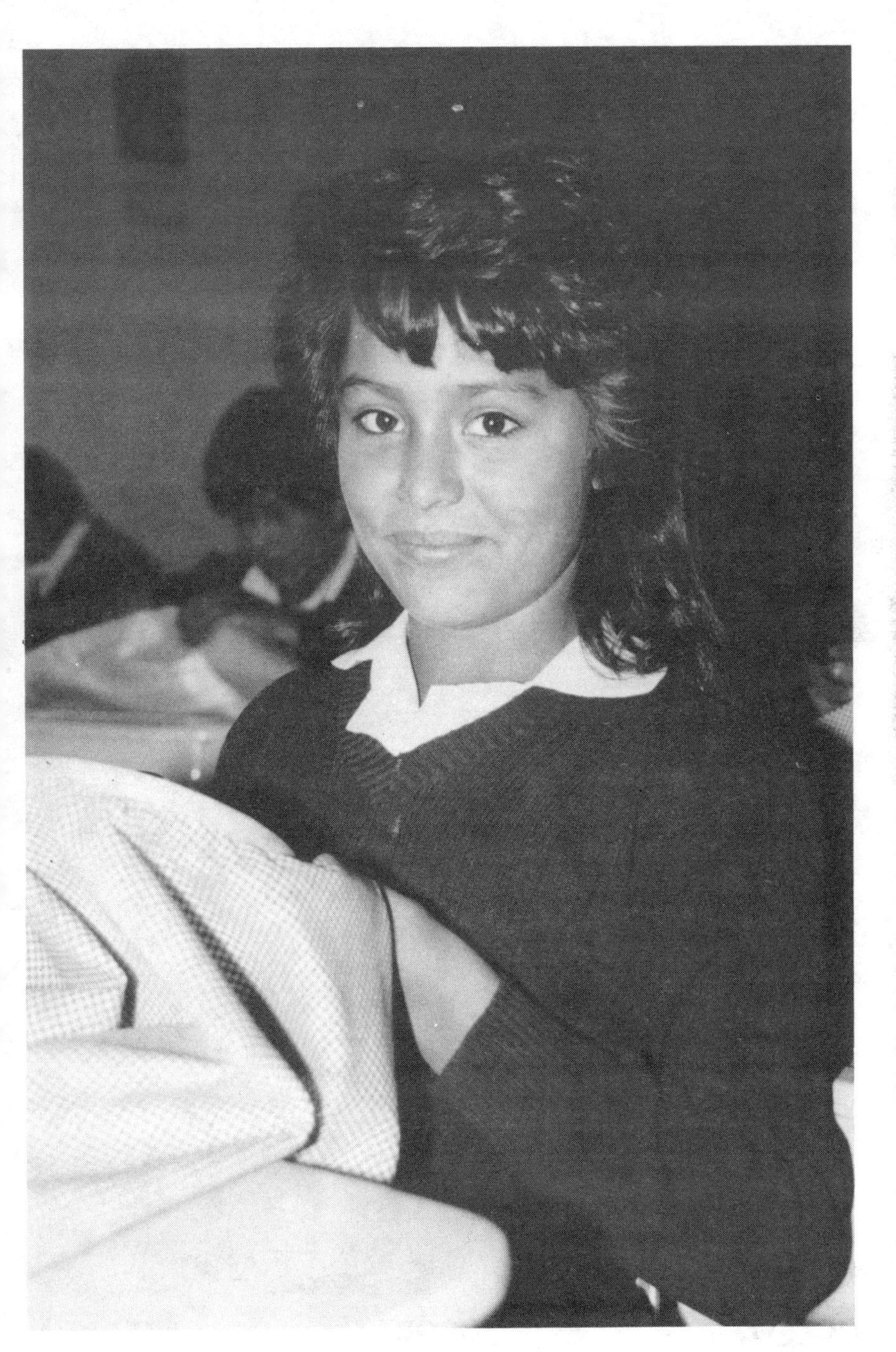

OLGA

OCTAVEO **JORGE** **HERBERTO**

CARLOS

HOME FOR
CHILDREN
Foundation for His
HOGAR
NIÑOS
ONE MILE

DAVID

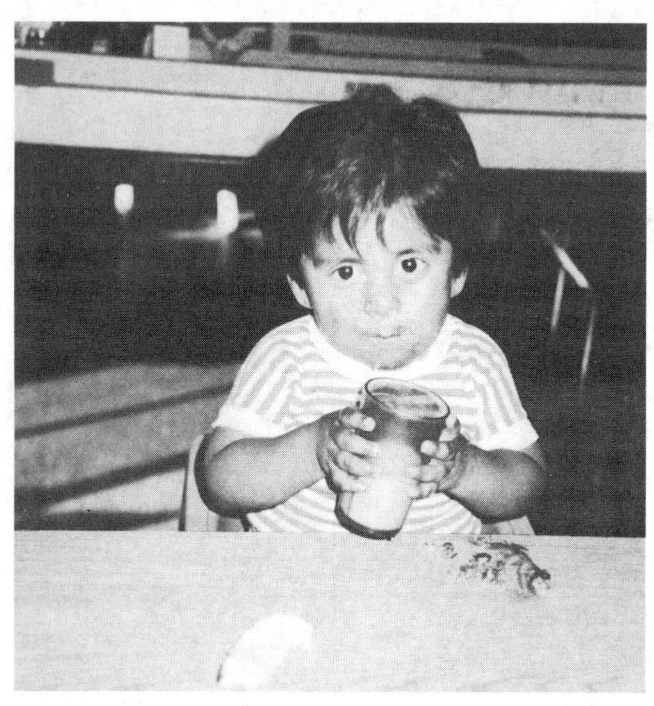

JORGE

DAVID

10

SHOES, PANTS AND CANNED MILK

The world's daily discords, too many things to do in too little time, and heavy concerns and worries sometimes dull our sensitivity to messages from God. Often I remind myself that we must attune ourselves to Him or, to put it in the words of the Psalmist, "Be still and know that I am God."

Thrilling miracles have sometimes occurred when I listened, heard and followed His guidance.

Once, shortly before a planned trip to the orphanage, I received a letter from my friend, Señora Martinez, which Chuck had translated by Mike Hammer, one of his Spanish-speaking friends.

She shared the news that she had just had a baby, and my heart raced with excitement, as I remembered how she had lost a baby.

Although she could nurse her infant this time, she desperately wanted canned milk as a back-up. Also, her husband needed a pair of pants and shoes, because he had a chance to get a job.

In the middle of the translation, Mike stopped, glanced up, and said, "I've got an extra pair of size nine shoes. Take them."

Chuck did, and when he arrived home and told me the contents of the letter, I felt the do-it-yourself side of me rise to the occasion, urging, *"Charla, why don't you grab Chuck's pants that he doesn't use and go to the the grocery store for a few dozen cans of milk?"* While rummaging through the closet, I got a sudden check from the Spirit. I thought, *"Oh, no, that's too still and small a voice . . .".*

Then I remembered that God seldom speaks in thunder and lightning so, I replied, "All right, God." Then, as I visualized Chuck's tall, slender build, compared with Señor Martinez' short, blocky physique, I laughed. Chuck's trousers would have had to be rolled back up toward Martinez' knees. Futhermore, Martinez had four to five inches too much waist for them.

The Lord always comes through with something better when he checks me, so my curiosity started to race. How would he handle my needs this time?

First I had to stop at the Montebello home of friends, Doc and Jan Higgins, to pick up Andrew Nichols, a young man from England who wanted to see the orphanage and do some odd jobs for us. One of the first things Jan said to me was, "Hey, Charla, Doc's on a diet and has lost a lot of weight. Can you use some men's pants?" She pointed to a pile of them to the right of the front door.

"Yes, I can!" and I told her about Señor Martinez, whose build was about the shape that Doc's had been. "Thank God for these gifts," I cried and told her and Andy how two of my three needs for the trip had already been filled without my having to ask anyone for them.

As Andy and I headed toward the border, I told God, *"I don't know how You're going to arrange for the canned milk, but I leave that to You."*

In San Ysidro, we stopped at a modest motel, where I often buy Mexican auto insurance. I was cheerfully greeted by a desk clerk whom I had known for some time.

"Hi, the usual policy," I told him, showing him my vehicle registration and handing over payment.

We completed the transaction, and as Andy and I started for the door, he called out, "Mrs. Pereau!"

I turned, thinking I had left something on the desk.

"Yes."

"Could you use some canned milk in Mexico?"

"Canned milk?" I was almost floored. "Did you say canned milk?"

"Yes," the clerk glanced quizzically at me. "Is something wrong?"

"No," I smiled, "everything couldn't be more right! Canned milk is exactly what I need!"

"Great," he replied, grinning. "You'll never believe how I happened to get them. Yesterday a man tried to take three cases of Carnation milk across the border to some mission, and the Mexican border officers wouldn't let him do it."

The clerk even helped us load the cases into the car. We thanked him and, overjoyed, drove across the border. God had provided everything I needed and, at the same time, He taught me a lesson: that sometimes I was supposed to be the channel of His supply, not always the source.

How important it is to listen, sense and obey the checks from God, I told myself. Immediately I recalled a remarkable incident which had occurred in the earliest years of the orphanage when I was teaching a women's Bible study group in Thousand Oaks on the gifts of the Holy Spirit.

These women were a tremendous blessing and

encouragement to the orphanage as well as donors of supplies. Each year they gave a Christmas party, inviting in neighbors and friends for prayer and refreshments. Those who came brought gifts for the children at Guerrero.

One Wednesday morning I woke up early, full of urgency that I was supposed to go to Mexico. "I don't know why, Chuck, but I know I'm supposed to go today."

He glanced curiously at me. "You rarely do in the middle of the week."

"That's right." Chuck had long since grown accustomed to my intuitions from the Lord and shrugged his shoulders.

"Fine, but please leave soon so that the daylight doesn't get away from you. I don't want you driving the bad part of the road after dark. That makes me worry."

"No, I won't." He kissed me goodbye and left for the fire station. As I was about to gather up some groceries and throw a change of clothes into a brown paper bag, my Tijuana Samsonite — I felt a strong check from the Lord. Apparently, I wasn't supposed to leave immediately.

That was all right with me. I made beds, prepared the evening meal for the family and alerted my neighbor Bev to check on the children during my fast trip to Mexico.

Now it was nine o'clock, and my promise to Chuck not to dally made me move. Why had the Lord checked me? I was not sure. Just as I was about to leave, the sharp ring of the phone startled me. It was Ann Mills, one of the women in the Bible study group.

"Charla," she said, "Barbara had a dream last night that the orphanage was out of food. She phoned Joanne Morrill, told her, and Joanne had a witness in the Spirit that Barbara was right."

I began to tingle, because what she said tied into my own input from the Lord.

"Charla, we and the others in the Bible study group gathered up funds and are going shopping at the supermarket. If we bring food to you, is there any way to get it down to Guerrero?"

"Absolutely," I said. "I'm ready to go."

Two hours later, a station wagon stopped in front of the house, loaded with dry milk, flour, beans and canned goods. We transferred it, I thanked them, and headed away. God's check had held me in the house until the phone call.

Sure enough, when I pulled in at the orphanage I found that the cupboard was bare. All the food had been eaten that evening. I felt two warring emotions. Annoyance that such a thing could happen and praise and admiration for God's supply — for answering the need before we even knew for certain that it existed.

11

SE VENDE (FOR SALE)

A strange uneasiness troubled me. Something was wrong at the orphanage. I could sense it all the way from North Hollywood.

I had made a number of south-of-the-border trips to deliver twenty beds which Pepperdine University had given us for the orphanage. Al Ottum, a friend had heard that Kern Foods Inc., was changing lids on its jars of jelly and was able to get a donation of 500 jars of jelly with the old type lids. I had brought them to Guerrero.

Three weeks later, I drove down there again. When we ate, no jelly was served, and there were no jelly-jar drinking glasses around.

Was it right to question how or where gifts given were used? I tried to suppress my doubts and nagging questions. Why hadn't the field been plowed and planted with beans for food for the children? Chuck gave the money for that project on our last trip.

Face to face confrontation has never been easy for me. I'd rather face an angry dog than an angry friend. I could always think of enough scriptures to reinforce my position.

"Love bears all things, believes all things, hopes all things, endures all things." I Cor. 13:7.

Romans 14:13 "Don't judge one another. Let us pursue the things that make for peace and building up of one another."

I believe it would be easier for me to walk on water than to sit on the board and debate the theology on that subject with doubting friends.

Distractions, often painful ones like the coming of new orphans or abandoned children, usually sidetracked me from probing. I had been overwhelmed with sadness and sympathy when a social worker from Ensenada, Josefina Barajas, brought us two little children found eating garbage in a dump there.

Rosa, the seven-year-old, was one of the most pitiful sights I had ever seen. Her hollow, near-skeleton's face held overbright brown eyes and black hair in a butch haircut with dandruff-caked scalp. A pot belly protruded from her skinny frame.

Her four-year old brother Angel, crippled by polio and suffering from rickets and extreme malnutrition, was attached to her like a little monkey, his misshapen, bony arms and legs wrapped around her body.

My heart went out to them. Their pain was my pain.

"Oh, God," I whispered to myself, *"Show me how to help them."*

Rosa shyly told Josefina that "Angel can move without help by pulling himself along the ground with one arm."

We could handle Rosa's needs at the orphanage, but how could we help Angel?

Without a birth certificate or other legal papers, we could not take him across the border for treatment. Then, too, who could pay the tens of thousands of dollars to get him the surgery and other treatment needed?

Later, when I described Angel's condition to Chuck, I could see his eyes mist. He talked to Walter Henry, a compassionate fellow fireman, who made Angel a personal project, got him legally across the border and into the Orthopedic Hospital and then the Shriner's Hospital for Crippled Children.

Through it all, God kept my vision for the orphanage burning brightly. Often when gazing across the 72 acres, I saw things to come as if they were already there — not just eleven happy, healthy, laughing children growing and learning in the Lord, but one hundred or more at a time and remodeled and new structures, plus an extensive orchard and gardens, a church and a Bible school.

In April, 1967, I shared this vision with Dave and Audrey Taylor. Both of them became excited about the plan and purpose, particularly Dave, who soon rearranged his working schedule at the drug store to drive down to Guerrero and look the place over. No sooner had he returned than he phoned me.

"Charla, I don't know exactly what it is, but something's radically wrong down there."

This troubled me, because I had the highest respect for Dave's discernment and keen ability to evaluate a situation. The picture became a little more clear a few months later, at the end of June, when Chuck and I made special arrangements with the American Consulate to bring eleven orphanage children to Family Bible Camp at Crestline for a week.

The springs in our nine-passenger station wagon creaked under so many of us mashed in with bedrolls and a week's supply of clothing. At the border, a U.S. immigration officer, a large man in his mid-fifties, with tanned skin, a square chin and brown, tortoise shell glasses, approached us.

I told him our destination and passed over documents which I had secured from the American Consulate to enable the children to cross into the United States.

"I'm taking these children to Family Bible Camp," I told him. Seeing us sardined in, he grinned in a fatherly way and commented, "That is *really* a full house!"

We both laughed, he waved us across, and I thanked him. None of the children had ever been in a big city, and I drove on freeways through Los Angeles before heading for North Hollywood. It was now twilight, and the electric lights of Los Angeles started to come on. These children from the world of kerosene lamps had never before seen entire buildings illuminated and they chattered all at once, pointing, nudging one another and exclaiming. This was more than just the first view of a metropolis to them. It was like a sudden birth on a new planet.

Tall buildings fascinated them. As they peered upward, a boy named Ramon repeated, "Mira! Mira!" (Look! Look!). Another child cried out, "El Banco." (A Bank). "It's full of money," added a little girl. A boy named Jorge yelled, "If the Americans have so much money, why don't they buy another sun and hang it in the sky so we could be warm at night, too?"

The children weren't the only excited ones. Their driver was, too, because she was receiving a fresh view of the old city through their eyes. Family Bible Camp also charged them up. They liked their Spanish-speaking teacher and talked freely to him and among themselves in his presence. After the first two days, their teacher came to Chuck and me in concern and, lowering his voice, confided, "When we can talk privately, I have something very important to tell you."

"How about right now?" asked an alarmed Chuck, and we three found a secluded bench.

"Either these are the biggest liars in the world, or there are unbelievable problems at the orphanage." Then he told us what the children were saying. "Very little of the clothing and supplies which you send down to Guerrero ever gets to the children. It's being sold, and only God knows what else is going on!"

Now my mind raced back to the missing jars of jelly, beds, and a big sign written in Spanish I had seen on the front door. "Se Vende" (for sale) How could we have been so stupid?

As we thought back to subtle irregularities, we realized why we had not made an issue of them. Although we had visited Guerrero often, we hadn't spent much time there, mainly due to Chuck's job and our responsibilities at home. Further, we had ignored our spiritual discernment, wanting to believe all things, suppressing pointed questions as criticisms. Love is not critical. We didn't want to judge. But my feelings contradicted my faith and I said to Chuck, "Let's take the children back to Guerrero and forget we have ever been there."

12

THE ENEMY INDIFFERENCE

I ached inside as we drove away from the orphanage. Oh, I wish I hadn't understood little Rosa's question. "Will you come back? Will you also leave me?" I cried for myself, I cried for His little ones.

Yet we had to face the facts. Although we provide some support we had no say in the administration. This wasn't our country or land and the children were not ours.

Driving north we had a choice of roads — the high road with it's rocks and ruts — or the low road a foot deep in powdery dust which would engulf the whole car and obscure our vision.

But we were confronted with a far greater decision. Forget? Can one forget? Should we forget? Do we turn our backs and drive north? Forget we ever visited Colonia Guerrero? Is forgetting equal to indifference?

Indifferent — Jesus was never indifferent. I picked up my Bible which some times resembles a filing cabinet. I carry it with me just about everywhere. I remembered writing something on that subject on the back pages.

Indifference is a besetting sin, the epitome of evil in our day. The opposite of love is not hate — it's indifference. The opposite of faith is not heresy — it's indifference. The opposite of life is not death — it's indifference. Because of indifference one dies before one actually dies. Faith doesn't look at the facts. It looks to God, "the Father to the fatherless", Psalm 68:5.

A possible solution came to us. We had learned that the orphanage was being given partial support with funds from a church in southern California. We would talk to the minister of that church. After hearing about the problems, he would certainly take corrective action. I turned out to be wrong. His first reaction was, "That's Mexico. Que sera, sera!"

I couldn't believe it. Noting my surprise, he continued. "Mrs. Pereau, ministering this church is both time-consuming and stressful. There's not much else we can do about peripheral things. We're already spread too thin."

While I sympathized with him and his local problems, I was troubled by his unwillingness to correct a situation for which he had administrative responsibility. If we talked in greater depth and I let him know of our dedication, perhaps he would change his mind and straighten out the situation.

So I questioned him and, in the process, learned much about the history of the abandoned buildings, the orphanage and homely, flat-roofed church.

In 1923 the owner of the Colonia Vicente Guerrero property struck upon the idea of capitalizing on wealthy guests at the nearby Hamilton Dude Ranch. He built a gambling casino with cantina and a motel-brothel.

Right after World War II, the United States and Mexican governments planned a vast hydro-electric project in the rocky canyon overlooking Colonia Vicente Guerrero to turn desert waste into acreage for growing and to supply electric power to Baja. Part of the plan was to build a paved highway from California. Laborers and tourists would bring business and prosperity to the area.

Señor Refugio Gomez, who owned the property, was well into constructing a two-story, concrete block theater for motion pictures and girly shows, when Washington cooperation fell through. Money had been appropriated but somehow never was disbursed. Gomez, disgusted and considerably less wealthy, abandoned his plan and the buildings, moving to Ensenada.

In 1963, while escorting friends around the Baja Peninsula, a retired minister, Alexander Brody, and his wife had stumbled upon the Gomez development. Immediately he had a vision of an orphanage, a vision with sound, like I had had — the laughter of children from one of the buildings and fields of waving grain.

My skin prickled with excitement.

Brody had knelt and claimed the property for the Lord. Later he had talked the southern California minister in whose office I was seated into paying $100 a year to lease the property and $100 a month toward orphanage expenses.

Although Brody had personally hauled whitewashed laths, plywood and other lumber from a dismantled Army barracks in Costa Mesa (now the site of Southern California College) and built the chapel, he felt too old to run an orphanage and left the job to others.

The church never felt a deep obligation to the Guerrero orphanage. Grafted onto its major missionary programs, the orphanage could not receive all the attention required. Persons or couples selected as directors proved unsatisfactory, contributing to increased disillusionment of the church.

I was shocked to learn that, during a visit to Guerrero, Pastor Brody discovered that the man then directing the orphanage was a secret alcoholic. Angered at the possibility of exposure, the director struck Brody on the head, knocking him unconscious for many days and blinding him. Pastor Brody never recovered his eyesight.

Historically, the orphanage had brought a large number of serious problems and concerns to the church, while caring for only a small number of homeless children. Its marginal success was not encouraging to a sponsor. Yet, why couldn't someone be found to take full responsibility to shape up the place? I left with that persistent question going around in my mind.

13

HENRY'S HOST, AN ANGEL

During this time, Angel had been in the hospital in Los Angeles, recuperating from extensive major orthopedic surgery. He then had to endure almost three months of a half-body and leg casts. The pain and discomfort were real for this little four year-old stranger in a foreign country.

Perhaps the greatest pain was separation from his sister. Several times each day his soft brown eyes would become pools of tears. Through tight lips he would speak the only word that Walt and Marge Henry could understand, "Rosa". It's hard enough to comfort your own child going through this kind of an ordeal, but with the language barrier, homesickness and physical pain, there was little consolation.

At last the day came when Angel and Rosa would be reunited. He wouldn't run to greet her, but for the first time in his life he could stand upright and walk with the help of leg braces and crutches. Walt, who was also on the A shift on the Fire Department, gave us a call. "Charlie, I know you're kind of disillusioned about the ministry in Mexico, — Mexican burn out — but how about riding along with me to take Angel back? It will be a long trip without anyone to talk to." "OK, I've got a couple of days off.

This should be quite a reunion." One hour later they were headed south on the 14-hour journey home for Angel. Chuck and Walt had made many trips together. They spent the hours singing together and memorizing hymns.

Angel watched out the car window relentlessly in hopes of seeing something familiar. Finally, in disgust, he said, "Carros, carros, carros, casas, casas, casas", (cars, cars, cars, houses, houses, houses) and laid down on the back seat and went to sleep.

It was late afternoon before the bomberos (firemen) reached the creek at San Vicente, Mexico. They had to ford about a foot of water between the steep embankments. When they reached the other side they were stopped by a Mexican bandit. He looked like he had stepped out of the movie "The Treasure of Sierra Madre". He was dressed in white, bullet belts, banderoles, across each shoulder and a large sombrero with tassels that bobbed as he turned his head and he had a bayonet affixed to his already long rifle. Chuck wanted to step on the gas but was afraid to move. The bandito stepped up to the open car window and growled, "Have you got any money?" Walt sat in stunned silence. Chuck answered "No sir, just enough to get us to the orphanage in Guerrero and back home." "Got any cigarettes?" "No sir, sorry, we don't smoke." In the full grip of fear, Chuck's heart pounded, wondering what his inquisitioner's next question would be. Walt was praying. To the amazement of both of them, the road-side bandit granted, "A paso", and motioned them on. When they reached the top of the hill they looked back. The bandit's compadres, mounted on horses, were riding around in a circle whooping it up. Walt broke his vigil of silent prayer. "Charlie, was that for real or divine intervention? But then we had an 'angel' in, the back seat."

For four more numbing hours they drove.

At the orphanage something was radically wrong. There was no one in sight. No welcoming committee. Usually the children ran out to greet visitors, especially these bomberos (firemen). Usually they joyously exclaimed, "Chack, Chack" and looked for a big hug and some goodies. But the anticipated blessed and happy reunion turned into an evil nightmare.

The buildings had all been vacated. All the furnishings, clothing, food, everything but trash was taken. Two dogs and a goat had been left shut in the building to starve. One of the dogs was dead. The other two animals were too far gone to be spared. Stunned, grief-gricken, sickened, the men put the dying animals to sleep. A few hours later they got back in the car and drove the long desolate route north in bewildered silence.

It wasn't our country. We didn't own the property and they were not our children. This heinous situation had to be reported to someone, but to whom, I asked myself. We couldn't just sit in North Hollywood unconcerned. Something had to be done.

I phoned Bea Peterson to put her on standby to watch over the children and packed a change of clothes for still another trip south — this time alone. Visions of the children crowded my mind. I thought about dear little Rosa. Thank God little Angel was safe in Granada Hills with the Henrys.

Driving through Ensenada, I saw the Palacio Municipal. That was the place to make my report, if I could find an interpreter. After numerous futile attempts, I finally located a woman who understood and spoke English. She listened to the hideous facts and said, "I shall take you to someone who can help."

Who should that person be but Josefina Barajas, the social worker who had brought Rosa and Angel to Guerrero? Striking, in a dark dress with white trim, she stood erectly to her five foot six height to greet me. Her high cheekbones and fine brown skin added distinction to her appearance of strength and dignity.

I told it all through my interpreter, letting her know that I would do everything humanly and prayerfully possible to find the children.

At every detail, Josefina Barajas reacted with controlled anger which showed in flashing, dark eyes and machine-gunned interjections. There was no doubt in my mind that the proper authorities would hear the whole story and be alerted to the missing children.

"Señora Pereau, it would be wise for you to check all orphanages between Tijuana and Guerrero and talk to the Delegados of the many ejidos, leaving them names and descriptions of the children. Searching from house to house would be impossible."

We shook hands and she wished me good fortune. I left with the impression that this dynamic woman, a champion of the underprivileged, who had helped the cause of the orphanage directly and indirectly on many occasions, was destined to rise far higher than her present position. I was pleased that she later became Mexico's first woman senator.

Every weekend for three months, I searched for the children. Several times Josefina Barajas arranged to have interpreters accompany me. Finally, as we drove many backroads, I found the first missing one — a seventeen year old youth — walking alongside a narrow dirt road. He had been sleeping in an abandoned, wrecked car, dirty and shoeless, subsisting on birds he could trap and wild honey. He had left the orphanage on his own and knew nothing about where the other children were.

Three others were in a Tijuana orphanage. I was overjoyed that they were well and being cared for and left them there to continue the search for the others. I followed Josefina Barajas' plan, talking to Delegados of the villages and following their leads. I enlisted various persons to go with me.

One day with Reverend Fred McCall, a licensed Lutheran pastor and his wife Mickey, from San Clemente, I learned from Pidgin-English questioning that there was an orphanage on the Tecate Road. In their white, 4-door Mercedes we pursued leads for much of the day, — tired, perspiring, hungry and thirsty.

"We have to be back in San Clemente before dark," he reminded me. Already the sun was low in the sky and even if we had started then, we wouldn't have made it in time.

"Would you mind taking me down this road?" I pleaded. He glanced sharply at me and said "There's no way we can cover every back road and burro trail in Baja."

"Can't we try just one more?" I asked.

Reluctant, but then with resignation, he drove eastward toward Tecate. For many miles we bounced and jostled over the narrow, winding, pot-holed road past dusty, olive drab chapparal without seeing a sign of life, even a buzzard.

Then at San Antonio crossing, I spotted a crumbling adobe hut about 350 feet off the road. "Will you stop for a few minutes?" I asked, and he did. Mickey and I stepped out and trudged toward the hut, where we found an old, stooped, toothless woman with leathery, wrinkled, brown skin. A red, white and grey bandana covered her head with wisps of white-grey hair protruding from the sides.

"Is there an orphanage around here?" I asked in my sad Spanish.

She brightened. It surprised me that she understood and said, "Si," pointing a bony finger of her dark brown-spotted hand in an easterly direction.

As we turned and started back to the car, Mickey asked, "Charla, did you see that little girl at the side of the house staring at you?"

"What girl?" I whirled around and, sure enough, there, in a dirt-spotted, red, cotton dress, her shaved head covered with red ringworm, was Rosa. My eyes caught hers, and she cried out, "Hermana" (sister), and we ran to one another and hugged.

"Rosa, Rosa," I cried out again and again.

As tears rolled down her cheeks, she said in Spanish, "I knew you would find me." All the while, the old woman looked on in bewilderment. She could not figure out the connection between Rosa and me. Perhaps she was thinking, "What is this rich American woman with the beautiful car doing here? How does she know Rosa?"

Rosa looked up at her and tried to explain. Over and over, she told the woman that I was "Hermana buena" (a good sister).

Already the sun was down, pastor Fred was due in San Clemente, and I had to return to North Hollywood.

I bent down to Rosa and took both of her grimy hands into mine.

"Rosa, listen to me. I will be back for you. Do you understand?"

She nodded.

On the way through Ensenada, we stopped briefly at the Palacio Municipal, where I told Josefina the location in which we had found Rosa. She was elated and promised to pick up the child and put her into the best Ensenada orphanage, where I could see her. Angel and Rosa would soon be reunited. We had found nine of the eleven children safe and secure. How relieved and hopeful I felt as we neared the border.

As I lay on my bed that night I thanked our heavenly Father over and over, then asked, *"Now what?"*.

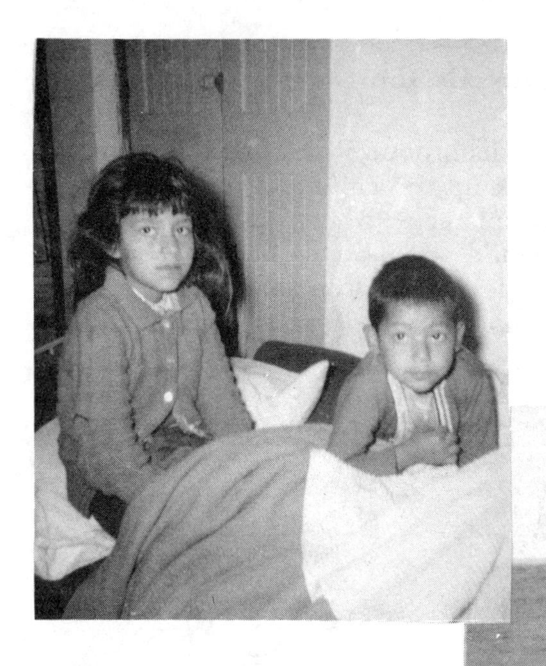

ANGEL, ROSA AND WALT HENRY

14

NOW WHAT?

Señor Refugio Gomez, owner of the deteriorating abandoned property had decided to put it on the market. Soon squatters and derelicts would take possession. Rather than risk losing everything he took quick action.

I had claimed the property for the Lord.

"God, don't let anybody jump that claim!" I pleaded.

Quickly, I alerted Dave Taylor to the danger, and we arranged an appointment with the American minister who held the lease on the orphanage land and told him what was happening.

Apprehension haunted Dave Taylor and me. The Guerrero property belonged to the Lord for His homeless children. We didn't want it to fall into the wrong hands and be put to commercial use. We spent hours with the minister, pleading with him.

"Please buy the land," Dave urged, "If you don't it's going to be sold, and who knows what the next owner will do with it?"

This did not seem to bother the minister. "We have a valid lease on the property. Besides, who would want it?"

"It's valuable property," countered Dave. "You

can't find another piece of land of that quality in the Guerrero area — 72 fertile acres in that arid country, a pure water well and four buildings. All of that is on the market for just $15,000 - only $5,000 down."

The minister shook his head.

"Sorry, I'm not led to buy it."

"But . . . " I cut in.

"Investing in Mexico is like pouring water down a rat hole," he interrupted.

"If you buy the property, I'll help you raise the money," I offered.

He shook his head. "As I've told you, we have a valid lease."

"Leases don't mean much in Mexico," I replied.

"Be that as it may, I do not feel led to purchase the property."

That troubled Dave and me. A contractual agreement between a U.S. citizen and a Mexican is usually not worth much more than the paper it's written on.

"I know that God's work is to be continued at Guerrero," I told the minister. "If you aren't led to make this step of faith, God will raise up someone else. That property is going to be a lighthouse in the darkness of the Baja Peninsula."

That ended the session but not Dave's and my determination. With more free time than Dave, I called on a succession of Christian organizations such as World Vision and large churches to interest them in buying property as an orphanage and was given a polite audience but little more.

Than I called on Don Moomaw, dynamic pastor of the Bel Air Presbyterian Church, a warm, gracious and loving person. This super-busy man listened as if he had all day. I told him everything, starting with the vision on my first visit to Guerrero to my vision of an orphanage for more than 100 children, a Bible school, trade school to equip the youth for earning a living and a mission center.

Pastor Moomaw's eyes glowed with appreciation.

"You have a great plan. I wish we could back you, but unfortunately our church is not large enough to handle something that extensive. So far as the orphanage is concerned, I feel that no one has the vision that you have. If God gives you the vision, He will give you the implementation."

He ended our meeting with a prayer. I shall be eternally grateful to Pastor Moomaw. Of the many organization and church individuals I had spoken to, he was the only one to give me human and scriptural encouragement. More than that he gave me the revelation that perhaps Chuck and I were supposed to assume the responsibility for buying the property.

Chuck and I called a meeting of our prayer group on the following Sunday. They all were familiar with our vision for the property and had already contributed to the orphanage in many ways. We had all fasted and prayed before getting together. Those who participated with us were Dave and Audrey Taylor, Walt and Marge Henry, Clayton and Mary Peterson and Richard and Sylvia Flaten.

Part of God's guidance was the reminder of the exciting things He had done through George Mueller. During the 19th Century, Mueller had shown unshakeable faith in God's ability to supply a building, food, clothing and all other requirements for orphans.

He had told no human being of the orphanage's needs — only God, and God supplied everything.

If God could do it *then*, He could do it *now.*

It was agreed that I should drive to Ensenada to talk to Señor Refugio Gomez about his property. I did and the meeting with him, a professing Christian, was a peculiar one. At times he seemed to like the idea of continuing use of the property for a Christian orphanage, then he would tilt in favor of commercial or industrial use.

"We have a prayer group praying that the property will continue as an orphanage," I informed him.

"I really want you to have it," smiled Señor Gomez. "I will give you three weeks to bring me the down payment of $5,000."

Then before leaving, I said, "If God provides money, I'll be back in three weeks."

Señor Gomez nodded and responded, "I am eager to sell as soon as possible. The first person here with the down payment, gets the property."

That was not much of a promise for us to go on.

At the next Sunday afternoon meeting of our prayer group-orphanage committee, we named Dave Taylor chairman.

The committee agreed unanimously that we should buy the property, as God provided.

"It's going to take fervent, unceasing prayer" I said, "because if we all pooled our liquid assets, we couldn't raise $5,000."

We adjourned to give more prayerful consideration to the project.

On the following Sunday, we went around the room for everyone's opinion. Should we go ahead with our plans and, if so, how? I remember saying, "If we go forward, we'll have to do battle with the Devil. It could cost us everything — our time, treasure and even our lives."

Each of us thought about that for a minute. I have never seen so many grave faces in one room. We all had our own responsibilities and financial commitments. *Should we commit ourselves?*

Audrey spoke up. "If we go down and erect a

cross on the property, used for so many of the Devil's purposes, we're going to do battle with the enemy."

We then went back to basics. The orphanage had to be saved, no question about that. Risk should have nothing to do with our decision, only faith.

"Let's put raising the money in God's hands," recommended Dave, who has a tremendous faith in the Lord for all things, particularly money.

Unanimously we decided to try Mueller's method. After all, God had brought us together in this cause, so he would deliver the money without our soliciting or publicizing our needs. Knowing that I would beg money for the orphanage, if necessary, the committee voted to rely on faith in God's provision. They could probably visualize me standing in front of the May Company with a tambourine in hand. Actually, everybody favored the faith method, because we wanted confirmation from God that the project and our participation in it were of God.

So we made a pact that if anyone asked us about the orphanage, we could tell him or her what was going on but we could not solicit. On the next day I visited a little shoe repair shop on Lankershim Boulevard in North Hollywood to leave some shoes and chat with Grandpa Jack, its owner, a longtime, faithful friend and a man of prayer.

"How are things going at the Baja orphanage, Charla?"

"I'm not sure, Grandpa Jack. We're seeking the mind of God as to whether we should buy the orphanage and run it ourselves. Will you pray for our guidance?"

The little Greek shoemaker set down a pair of men's black shoes and turned to me. His thick hair seemed a little more grey that day, his back a little more bent. Tears began to mist his clear grey eyes.

"I don't have to pray about that, for the Bible says true religion is to provide for the widow and the orphan."

He told me facts of his early childhood when orphaned in Greece, he had to beg for crusts of bread and was kicked and spat upon like a stray dog.

Grandpa Jack went to the cash register of his ramshackle shop, punched the "No Sale" key with a large-knuckled finger, pulled out a $100 bill and handed it to me. This was the first gift of faith — a sacrificial gift — toward purchase of the property. I had no idea where this man of modest means got the $100.00

Being in the presence of this simple, yet profound man, was like being in the presence of Jesus. His little shop was like a cathedral in the market place. Great men studied the Scriptures with Grandpa Jack, who worked directly from the Greek. I shall never forget how many times, after repairing my shoes, he would inscribe Bible quotes in Greek on the instep. Usually I would take them to a friend who could read Greek. One of his scriptural messages was translated, "Stand firm in faith and prayer. . .".

On a Saturday night before our option expired, I held a baby shower at my home for a friend. One of my guests was Nova Nordseth of West Los Angeles.

"What's new in Mexico, Charla?" she asked.

"Nova, the land is up for sale, and a group of us has an option. If God provides the money, His work will continue there."

Nova nodded in appreciation. "That's something I want to be a part of."

She pulled a checkbook out of her brown leather purse and wrote a check, which she folded over and handed to me. I was dying to read the amount but it would not have been in good taste, so I thanked her and put it into my pocket.

After the shower was over, I opened it and thrilled at the amount — $100. I thanked and praised the Lord for the gift. The glow was still there on Sunday morning at eight when Nova phoned.

"Charla, that check I wrote for $100." "Yes?" I responded, afraid that she had reconsidered.

"When I wrote that, the first figure that came to mind was $200, then I reasoned that $100 was certainly a generous gift."

I was still hanging in suspense.

"Charla, I believe that the Holy Spirit wanted me to give $200. So I'm putting another check in the mail to you."

"Thank you, Nova. God bless you!" I said, my heart soaring up into the blue.

On that Sunday afternoon, Sylvia Flaten, appointed treasurer of our committee, told us good and sad news. People who had caught the vision —family, close friends and others who knew committee members — had given to the hilt, yet we were still $1,100 short and only a day away from the end of our option period.

Telling about Nova's phone call that morning, I said,

"Another check for $100 will be in the mail to me tomorrow."

"Even with that, we'll still be a thousand short," replied Sylvia.

Everybody seemed to be thinking about what I said. "We need a miracle."

Our spirits sagged. How sad if we had to return each contribution with a letter of thanks and acknowledgement that we had failed. Disheartened, we wondered, "Why had God let us down? Was this His way of telling us He was not behind the project?"

Nobody wanted to face that possibility, and we adjourned. When Monday's mail, including Nova's letter, arrived in the early afternoon, I tossed it all on the kitchen counter unopened. Twenty-four hours before, I had been thrilled with her promise of a second check. Now, although thankful for her generosity, I thought, *"It's just one more check I'll have to send back."*

After finishing my domestic chores, I sat down with a cup of coffee to open the day's mail. A note fell out of Nova's envelope and fluttered to the floor. I picked it up and read:

"Dear Charla, as I was writing the enclosed check, I was moved by the Holy Spirit to make it for this amount. I feel the new figure is what you require to complete the transaction. Love, Nova."

Deeply curious, I pulled out the check. When I saw the amount, I was almost bowled over. It was made for exactly what we needed to close the deal — $1,100.

Nova's letter and check had been mailed from Los Angeles on Sunday morning — many hours before the committee had even the remotest idea of the specific sum needed to complete the transaction. It was two-thirty. I would have to move fast. Hurriedly I phoned Dave Taylor to share the great news, then Sylvia Flaten, arranging to meet her at the bank to deposit Nova's check.

Now it was just after three o'clock. Even if I started for Ensenada immediately, I could never make it in time to meet Senor Gomez at a decent hour. Perhaps if I reached his office by phone, he would extend our option to the next day. Quickly I dialed the number. When the connection was complete, the phone rang — and rang — twelve times and no one answered. Frustrated, I hung up.

Maybe he was at home. I had no home number for him and dialed information, requesting his number. I could hear the operator flipping pages. Finally, she informed me that there was no residential listing for Señor Refugio Gomez.

All I could do was start for Ensenada early the next morning, hoping it would not be too late. I did.

On the drive south, I had to restrain myself from pushing the car's accelerator to the floorboard. The miles flew by, not only because of my speed but also because I was exhilarated. My vision was getting off the ground, not through some organization or church with a dispassionate interest but through our own home-made committee to whom the project was a labor of love.

I had no trouble finding the home of Señor Gomez. His wife answered the door and, smiling sweetly, said "Señora Pereau, my husband is not at home. He is at the office of his attorney."

I began to feel uneasy. *Attorney! Was he completing a deal with somebody else?* Mrs. Gomez gave me an address on Calle Ruiz, which I jotted down on the back of an envelope and made my way through frustrating traffic to Calle Ruiz. After weaving around double-parked cars and making almost endless circles around the block, I found a just-vacated parking spot.

In the attorney's outer office, a counter separated visitors from the inner sanctum. There I told a secretary-receptionist my name and asked if Señor Refugio Gomez was with the attorney.

"Si," she replied, wrote my name on a piece of memo paper and took it to the inner office. A minute later, she invited me through an opening in the counter to the attorney's office.

After a cordial greeting, Señor Gomez said, "Que lastima! (What a pity!) You weren't here yesterday, Mrs. Pereau, so I have already accepted an offer of $20,000 for the property. We are now preparing legal papers for the buyer, who wished to turn it into a hunting lodge for tourists."

A hunting lodge! I felt numb all over. Only minutes ago I had known the heights of exhilaration. Suddenly I was in the depths of despair. A vision had died before my eyes.

I stood there dumbly for I don't know how long with Gomez and the attorney staring at me. I couldn't believe what I was experiencing. It couldn't be true; yet it was. Then, almost in tears and numb, I turned and walked out of the room and past the counter.

"Blessed Lord, why did You let this happen after all our prayers? And why after You gave us the miracle for $5,000?"

"You are an American, are you not?" I was startled by a rich baritone voice speaking precise English. Glancing in the direction of the voice, I saw a middle-aged man in khaki pants and shirt, somewhat heavy for his five foot nine height. As I noted his greying hair and kind face, I realized that he was of Spanish ancestry.

"Yes."

"Tell me, what are you doing here?" Still about to burst into tears and not wanting to cry in public, I hesitated for an instant.

"I came from California to place a deposit to purchase some land but was too late. The property has just been sold."

"Where is this property? In Ensenada?"

At a loss to understand his interest, I replied, "No, about 110 miles south of here in Colonia

Vicente Guerrero."

Now he appeared to be even more curious.

"What do you want with property down there?"

At this point I got a grip on my emotions and thoughts. *Maybe I could share my faith with him!*

"It was not just I. I feel God wanted a home for needy children, a trade and a Bible school and a Christian mission center there."

My vision for the property came out in a rush of words. Patiently he listened, then asked, "Well, what happened?"

"Somebody else bought the property out from under us. According to the owner, Señor Gomez, the buyer plans to turn it into a hunting lodge for tourists."

Then he invited me to sit on a chair.

"I have made an *offer* on that property," he said, as I sat down. He talked rapidly in Spanish to the secretary and walked through the opening in the counter to the inner office. Within a matter of minutes, Señor Gomez and the man came out.

"Mrs. Pereau, I want you to know that Mr. Vela is no longer interested in the property and believes that you are supposed to have it. It is now available to you and your group under the original agreement."

"It's a deal, Señor Gomez," I beamed, thanked a smiling Mr. Vela, and fumbled in my purse for the checkbook. I was flying so high I could hardly write.

The vision was reborn and Mr. Vela became president of the Mexican corporation which holds title to the land.

15

ALL ABOUT ABEL

Crises have a way of coming in their own time. Had we a choice, we would have decided that it was not the right time for a new crisis.

This crucial problem revolved around Abel Gomez, the 17-year old son of a Ruben Jaramillo woman who had 23 children. One of the young people who had spent a week at Family Bible Camp, Abel had come into a personal relationship with Jesus there and his life was dramatically changed.

On the way to Guerrero, I would pick him up and bring him to the orphanage, where he worked eagerly and conscientiously. Abel developed an insatiable craving to learn to read.

He seemed to live for the evenings when we would discuss the Bible in the yellow light of the kerosene lamp. He tried again and again to read and, finally, one night, the words on the printed page of a Spanish Bible came through to him in a burst of illumination.

How well I recall the occasion when we gave him a Spanish Bible. Never before had he owned anything of value. All he could do was say, "Gracias, gracias . . .". Tears formed in his eyes, as he held and caressed his Bible.

Back in his hovel in Ruben Jaramillo, he studied the Bible by candlelight until the candle burned out and wisps of smoke trailed upward. Never have I seen a young man more qualified by sheer desire for the ministry. *"He has a pastor's heart,"* I told myself.

Within less than six months, Abel was reading the Scripture quite well. "Oh, how I would like to go to school," he confided to me. That hunger showed in his earnest, brown eyes. We tried to enroll him in the local school and failed. His general reading ability was not yet quite high enough. Then we took him to a Bible School in Tijuana, where he was tested and failed. Once his reading proficiency was upgraded, he would be accepted.

We were all let down — especially Abel. Every door seemed temporarily closed. Where I least expected it, a glimmer of hope broke through — an opportunity that was to put him and me through a harrowing, suspenseful experience. I went on a retreat in Desert Hot Springs with very close friends, Al and Lorraine Sonnenberg.

With Abel uppermost in my mind, I told them about him.

"That gives me an idea!" responded Al. "There are bilingual classes in the Palm Springs area for migrant workers."

Every cell in my brain lit up. *"Maybe this was the answer!"*

Al talked on. "I have a contact with the high school there. If you can deliver Abel to Desert Hot Springs, he can live with us. Lorraine can help him with reading and writing."

My prayers of thanks were already rocketing heavenward and Al phoned the principal of the school in Palm Springs, explaining about Abel. As he listened to the principal's reply, his face broke into a broad grin. It was arranged! A new mid-term class was starting in three days. If we could get him there by then, he could enroll.

Now Abel could fill in his literacy gap and, at the same time, be blessed by living with a fine Christian couple.

My mind raced ahead of reality. Soon he would be able to enroll in the Tijuana Bible school and then become a pastor to his own people.

Encouraged, I drove back home and shared the exciting news. Chuck, Andrea, Craig and Dan were caught up in the excitement. It was like having a built-in rooting section.

Now I had to put the plan in motion. Unfortunately, neither Chuck nor Andrea could look after the boys at home. Chuck would be at the fire station for the next two days, and Andrea, with a full-time day job and a heavy schedule of evening studies at Life Bible College, was rarely at home. I was thankful that Howard and Jean Wedell volunteered to help and I threw a few things together for the trip.

As I combed my hair in the mirror, I had a strong urge to wear a unique gold-washed necklace made by a Zapotec Indian artist in Oaxaca, Mexico and given to me under unusual circumstances. I admired its delicate filigree work — fine intertwined wires that resembled lace. It has great sentimental value to me. "*Why take the chance of losing it?*"

I set it back in a jewelry case. A little while later, almost unconsciously, I took it out of the case and snapped it in place around my neck. My close friend, Mary Peterson, was available and offered to make the trip with me. There was plenty of room in the station wagon for the two of us and the load of food, clothes and bedding accumulated for the orphanage.

Before crossing the border at Tijuana, Mary and I

stopped at the U.S. Immigration Service office to learn the right procedure for bringing Abel across. A courteous clerk gave us an impressive list of "things to do." Mary and I did the same thing on the Mexican side in Tijuana. Part of the time, I had an interpreter, and part of the time he had to absent himself. Somehow we got over the language obstacle course and came away with the impression that the basic item we needed was Abel's birth certificate.

"*A simple matter,*" I thought. Certainly his mother had registered his birth. Later, at the orphanage, Abel told us that this was not so.

I closed my eyes to pray silently. Somehow, in his own mysterious way, God had to find a way to snip the red tape and get Abel into the United States. Obviously, Mary and I had to act in a hurry so that Abel could enroll on time for the mid-term.

The three of us piled into the station wagon and set out on the long, hazardous route northward to Ensenada and the Palacio Municipal.

Between the difficulty in understanding and communicating and the complications of bureaucratic requirements, we were shunted from one desk to another for endless hours, not achieving anything but a high level of confusion and frustration. Once when we were asked to secure certain official stamps to satisfy requirements, we bought Federal postage stamps and handed them over. The clerk broke into hilarious laughter.

Embarrassed and disheartened, I hadn't the remotest idea where to turn and just happened to see a sign, "Presidente", over one of the doors. Maybe my Spanish was a notch or two worse than Abel's English but that word spelled "president" — to me the top man in Baja California.

We weren't doing too well at the bottom, so I

decided to start at the top. Frustrated, desperate and believing we were in the will of God, I started for that door with Abel and Mary right behind me. When he understood my intentions, Abel gently grasped my arm and tried to stop me. "No, no Hermana," he appealed but I kept on going across a small foyer toward an inner door. A squat man, neatly dressed in an odd jacket and pants, stepped in our path and addressed excited Spanish to me.

"Sorry, I don't speak Spanish."

Then in good English, he inquired, "Where do you think *you're* going? This is El Presidente's office."

"Yes, I know. It is necessary for me to see El Presidente."

"What for?"

"For a most important reason."

His piercing brown eyes scrutinized my face, then they fell to my necklace, which he studied for an embarrassingly long time.

"That necklace — where did you get it?"

"Why in the world did he want to know that?" I asked myself, but answered, "It was a gift from a man from Oaxaca, Mexico."

"Yes, I know its origin, but how did you happen to come by it?"

"Well, Señor, I adopted a Zapotec Indian baby, who was with me in Padua Hills, California, when we met an Oaxacan Indian pottery maker, who immediately recognized my boy as a Zapotec and was intrigued. He wondered why an American family would have a Zapotec Indian and asked for an explanation. When I told him, he was appreciative of our concern about the plight of his people and insisted on giving me this necklace."

Still blocking my way, the man continued studying the necklace and, in admiration, commented,

"You know making such intricate jewelry is almost a lost art." I knew the necklace and my story had made quite an impression on him.

Then abruptly he changed the subject. "What do you want with El Presidente?"

I placed my hand on Abel's shoulder and said, "This is my close friend, Abel Gomez. I have to get him a border-crossing card, and he has no birth certificate."

He frowned and wagged his head from side to side. "Woman, that is impossible!"

"All things are possible with God," I replied. "This boy is called to the ministry, and God has prepared a place for him to study in the United States. I believe we are going to get there."

He looked at me as if I had lost my mind.

"There is only one man who can help you, that is El Presidente."

"Señor, that is exactly why I am here."

He shrugged his shoulders impatiently, "He is not here now. You come back at six o'clock."

I shot a glance at my watch. It was three-thirty, as Mary, Abel and I left to fill in time at the house of a friend. What the man had said was itching my mind for answers. "*Who ever heard of a president coming to the office at six P.M. — especially in Mexico. We'll return to the place and probably find it pitch dark. What did he know about El Presidente? Maybe he was just the janitor trying to get rid of us.*"

Doubts continued to gnaw at me when Abel, Mary and I got into the station wagon at about ten minutes to six bound for the office of El Presidente. I began to worship God in my prayer language.

After parking behind the dark Palacio Municipal, we tried the rear door, fearing it would be locked, and found it open.

Directly inside the door, as if expecting us, was the man we had met earlier. He smiled, ushered us into El Presidente's office, asked us to be seated and announced, "I shall act as the interpreter."

He introduced us to El Presidente, seated behind the desk. I drew in my breath. El Presidente was striking enough to be in front of Hollywood cameras, rather than behind a desk. Immaculate in a dark brown suit with sparkling white shirt and lighter brown tie, every strand of his black, wavy hair with greying sideburns in place and his mustache neatly clipped. He smiled warmly, his teeth as white as his shirt. I liked him immediately. When noting Abel's nervousness and awe at being in the same room with El Presidente, he put him at ease with a gracious, understanding smile. He spoke to him in Spanish for about seven or eight minutes, asking questions which Abel, still ill at ease, answered briefly. He addressed a remark to our interpreter, who translated it for me.

"Of course, you realize that this boy's birth has never been recorded."

I nodded. Then El Presidente took a pen from his desk stand and a sheet of official stationery from a drawer and spoke to Abel:

"Where were you born?"

"Michoacan, Señor Presidente," replied Abel.

"When were you born, Abel?"

He shot a desperate glance at me, then, "Señor Presidente, I do not know."

El Presidente tried another attack. "How old are you?"

Again Abel was puzzled. "Seventeen or eighteen — more or less," he responded.

"But you do not have a birthday?" questioned El Presidente.

"No, Señor."

The president flashed a quick smile. "Everybody has a birthday," he said. "How would you like this lady's birthday?"

El Presidente turned to me, still smiling.

"When is your birthday, Señora?"

"July 4th, Señor Presidente."

"Bueno," he replied, writing that birthdate and the year he estimated to be the proper one on the letterhead, signing and applying his official seal.

I thanked El Presidente and his aide and hurriedly checked the paper. Under Abel's birthdate were the words: "I have seen all of his documents and papers and find them to be in order."

Abel and I left flying high and I mused about El Presidente's wording. Sure, he had seen all of Abel's papers, because there were none. He had seen all we had to show him. I held the document tightly in my hand as if it were a passport to Heaven. This would get us into the U.S.

So the three of us sped as fast as we could to the border. At the U.S. Immigration checkpoint we pulled to a stop.

"What's his citizenship?" the officer asked.

"Mexican", I answered, "but I have a letter from the president of Baja. . .".

"I don't care if you have a letter from the President of Timbuktoo. This boy is not going across the border."

Hurriedly, I drew the letter out of my purse. "Here's that letter."

Refusing even to look at it, he said, "That doesn't carry any weight with us."

Disarmed, I said, "But. . ."

"That's it for tonight lady," he replied. "You'll have to come back in the morning and go through the American Immigration Officer. He has to have a green card or a permit."

Rain was beginning to fall as we followed a painted line, making a U-turn back to Mexico. We felt as dismal as the weather.

It had already been a long day and, although we had a little food left, I suggested we conserve that and the little money we had, just in case we needed cash to pay fees.

"Let's skip eating tonight and sleep in the station wagon in a safe place for all night parking — the lot of the old Caliente Race Track," I said. That was all right with Mary and Abel, so we drove there.

Sleeping bags are standard equipment in our wagon as well as blankets. Mary settled in the back, Abel in the middle under a blanket, and I in front. Over the peppering rain on the roof, I could hear Abel slipping off his shoes.

Suddenly a strong, stale odor assailed us.

"What's that smell?" Mary asked sharply. "Did somebody get sick?"

"Not yet," I replied. Abel didn't understand English, so I explained to Mary. "He hasn't had a shower in some time and he just took off his shoes."

We started to laugh hilariously. With the persistent rain, we could open the windows only a crack, to let in fresh air.

Abel probably didn't understand our hilarity or care, because he was already snoring. Mary and I literally laughed ourselves to sleep.

After next morning's breakfast of oranges and hard boiled eggs left from the previous day's lunch, we drove through a drizzling rain to the Mexican Consulate to apply for a passport. Almost a hundred others with the same idea had arrived earlier.

"We could be here for a week," I told Mary.

Moving quickly, squeezing and weaving my way,

with Mary and Abel right behind, I eased into the lobby, where I noticed a flight of stairs to second floor offices. "*The top Honchos have to be there,*" I reasoned. A black haired lady with smooth, olive skin and a sharply hooked nose gave us a "No Trespassing" look, mixed with outright resentment.

Before she could speak, I handed her the letter. She studied it for an instant, nodded, then called to a woman at the nearby desk, "These people have a letter from El Presidente."

She turned back to me and said, "It is necessary to have photographs."

"Muchas gracias," I replied, and we hurried downstairs and outside into pouring rain and across the street to a shop where they took passport photos and developed them in 20 minutes. We parted with more of our dwindling money. We were sopping wet and cold by the time we returned to the Mexican Consulate, our hair dripping.

We were given a temporary visitor's passport and then drove to the American Consulate. Shunted from one desk to another, we picked up typed papers and paid small fees for all services. When everything seemed to be in order, an official said, "He will need X-rays before he can be admitted to the U.S."

So we rushed to a nearby medical office, praying that our last amount of cash would be enough. Surprise of surprises, Abel was X-rayed and there was no charge. We were told the X-rays would be available in 20 days.

Twenty days! I couldn't believe it.

"If you will come back in three weeks, you will have his crossing card," a woman clerk told us.

"Three weeks?"I asked. Abel had to be in Desert Hot Springs by morning.

"Yes," replied the woman. "A 72-hour Tourist

Permit will be ready by then."

A man at an adjoining desk looked up from his paperwork and told me. "You can get an extension on that."

"Three weeks is an awfully long time," I remarked. "May I see an immigration official?"

"They're all busy," she responded, waving her hand toward approximately 20 men behind a long counter, talking, gesturing and examining papers.

"Look, I'm an American citizen, and I must see an immigration official. I have a desperate problem."

She shrugged, "I'm afraid you'll have to take a number like all the rest. But I doubt you'll be called today."

We took a number and settled into molded plastic seats in a long row. Casually I glanced from one end of the counter to the other. Then I did a doubletake.

There was a familiar face. No doubt about it, he was the man who had admitted me and a station wagon full of Mexican youngsters to attend Family Bible Camp not long before. He had seemed a compassionate type.

A spontaneous prayer came out of my mouth.

"Oh, Lord, let that man call *my number* before the office closes." Slowly, intermittently numbers were called but not mine. Now the clock said 4:45. Probably five was quitting time. Maybe the woman had been right that my turn wouldn't come today. Then a voice over the speaker called my number.

Joys of joys! And whose window was open but that of the man I had met. Quickly Abel and I went to the counter.

"Hi," I said to the man as I put our paperwork before him. "I would like to get this boy into the U.S. today."

When he looked up, I thought he recognized me.

Then that impression faded, as he curtly replied, "Well, our regulations call for a wait of 21 days."

"Yes, but this is very important. I know somebody in this office has the authority to sign this paper and let us through. It is either you or some other official."

My determination made him study me and in partial recognition, he said, "I believe I've seen you before."

"Yes, you have. Last summer I came through here with 11 Mexican children bound for a Bible camp. You were the officer who came up to our station wagon and admitted us."

He grinned. "Now I remember. They were packed in like sardines."

"There's only one this time," I laughed. He appraised Abel, then me and finally, the paperwork. with a shrug, he scrawled signatures on the paperwork and stamped over them. He half-smiled at me:

"You know, Mrs. . . ."

"Pereau," I added.

"Mrs. Pereau, there is no time stamped on these documents, as to when he entered the country. For your information, we wouldn't know how long he was in the country, but you understand, this is only a 72-hour permit."

"Yes, I understand that. Thank you very much!"

And across the border we went with another prayer miraculously answered.

Abel came through for us. After six months with Al and Lorraine Sonnenberg, he became very apt at reading and writing Spanish and at other subjects. He understood quite a lot of English and spoke it hesitantly. Later, he passed entrance exams at the Tijuana Bible Institute and justified our confidence by studying hard and scoring the second highest grade in his graduation class.

Soon after he was made associate pastor (an unsalaried position) of a church in La Mesa, a suburb of Tijuana. He found a full-time job in a furniture factory and took on the obligation of supporting his young brother and sister who had been in the orphanage.

Abel's young brother and sister are becoming well known. Their images — a youngster embracing his sister — are on letterheads and newsletters for Foundation For His Ministry, Orphanage at Colonia V. Guerrero.

During the torrential rain of 1978, Abel and the youngsters were flooded out of their living quarters. Like thousands of other flood victims, he and his sister and brother moved to a tent city of thousands of blue, 8' x 10' tents, where life was so primitive that they cooked on a five-gallon paint can supported by sticks over a fire.

On a trip to Tijuana with precious friends, Pastor Harald Bredesen, his wife Gen and Lt. Col. Bill Riddell and his wife Kay, we stopped to see Abel in Tent City. Knowing his serious financial condition, I took a $10 bill from my purse, which, with gratitude, he refused.

"Hermana Charla, I could never take money from your hands."

"But Abel, this is for your little ones."

"No, I could never take money from you. These children are my responsibility."

I was disappointed yet proud of Abel. His high sense of integrity and responsibility so impressed the Bredesens and the Riddells that Bill initiated a move by his and the Bredesen's prayer group in Escondido, California, which bought the lot where Abel's tent was pitched and organized a team — including Chuck

— to build a fine, three-bedroom, cement-block home for him and the youngsters. Not long ago Abel married a beautiful Mexican girl and Bill Riddell was best man. One of the proudest moments of my life was being a part of the wedding group.

16

THE DOUBLE CROSS

"Oh Lord, teach me patience in a hurry." I prayed.

I really needed it in the land of "Mañana", where people don't do today what they can put off until tomorrow.

Our orphanage committee couldn't wait to transfer title of the property to a Mexican Corporation which we had just formed, Hogar Para Ninos Necisitados (Home for Needy Children). We were eager to secure a license to operate the orphanage.

The government of Baja California seemed indifferent.

Day after day, I haunted the Palacio Municipal in Ensenada, a bleak, dirty-white, two-story, old Spanish building. Its poorly lit interior was even less inviting; wide, unswept hallways with too many human beings for too few wooden benches; yellow and brown mongrel dogs sniffing the dingy sticky walls; castoff, United States furnishings; stale, rebreathed air, intermingled with body odors. About the only artistic touches in the place were colorful paintings of recent Mexican presidents and most fascinating to me, the one of Benito Juarez, the nation's first president, whose features were similar to those of Charles

Curtis.

Each day the appropriate official who was supposed to be in was out.

Daily recitals of my problem to a black-mustachioed clerk got me nowhere. The clerk would nod his head with my every word, giving the impression that it would be possible to see the official. All the head-bobbing turned out to mean it would be *impossible.*

Each time I asked a direct question, I got an indirect answer.

"Will he be here by ten o'clock?"

Smiling agreeably, the clerk would answer, "Mas or menos," and teeter his right hand.

I became weary of his "more or less" answer. Next morning the official was not in by 10 A.M., noon or 2 P.M.

Mañana!

Through part of July and August — in the sapping, muggy heat — I went through seventeen Mañanas, sometimes making trip after trip from North Hollywood, at other times sleeping in the station wagon. How often I thanked the Lord for my dear friends the Liskums, Petersons and Wedells who helped Andrea (then at home for summer vacation) care for our children.

"Lord, won't tomorrow ever be here?" I asked.

Another night in the old sleeping bag in the back of the station wagon.

Through it all, I tried not to be discouraged and depressed by drawing upon my supernatural vision of the property — the sound of laughing children and green crops waving on the land.

What a period of learning, of realizing that a ministry started supernaturally often had to go through many trials and heartaches before fulfillment.

Then, one day, mañana became today. On September 1, 1968, we got legal title to the property and took possession on October 1. All supplies and equipment that hadn't been bolted down — and some that had — were gone. We would have to start from the bottom. Far worse was what we encountered in the main building and church — the sickening smell of death from corpses of two dogs and three goats which had been left there without water or food to dehydrate and starve.

God sent us a delightful and capable couple, Bill and Lee Vonhoff, our first directors under this new foundation and work. And what work! We had to start from scratch or below that. But how the saints (our committee and everybody they knew) rallied and gathered pots and pans, dishes, knives, forks and spoons, beds, sheets, blankets, chairs, tables and food.

We got a windfall from the naval Training Center in San Diego, thanks to Chief Boatswain's mate Richard Peterson: 14 surplus navy bunkbeds, mattresses, blankets and sheets. When Chuck and I finished piling it all on our pickup and securing it, our cargo towered nine feet in the air and hung over, so that people facetiously asked if there "was a truck under all that junk."

On our southward trip, we and friends — also in trucks and cars piled high with widely assorted household furnishings — looked like characters out of *The Grapes of Wrath* with everything they owned, escaping the dust bowl.

Many of our saints also served as volunteer workers to get us set up. Hardly had we finished the organized chaos of moving in when we were overjoyed to welcome five of our original children and nine more from the endless supply Josefina Barajas found.

I have no idea what we could have done without the day and night efforts of the Vonhoffs, who also brought us Rogelia, a teacher of children's evangelism classes from Juarez, Mexico, who helped with the children's education and performed domestic duties.

The Vonhoffs did the heavy pioneering work to re-establish the orphanage and, sadly, after several months Lee suffered a recurring problem — bleeding ulcers, making it necessary for them to leave with just Rogelia in charge. Desperately we looked for directors and desperation caused us to make mistakes. We hadn't yet gained an understanding that frantic human efforts would only bring us misfits, rather than matchups. We hadn't yet grasped what Jesus taught: "Pray ye the Lord of the harvest that He send forth laborers."

In San Fernando, we found a man named Luke with a wife and six children and hurried there to interview him. We mistook his willingness for capability. On December 1, we gave him petty cash, $100 in payment for a month, a pantry load of food and clothing, and felt secure that all was well.

Early on Christmas morning, Chuck, a close friend, Dorothy Wagner and I overloaded our truck with a lot of furniture, food supplies and a holiday treat: cooked turkeys and trimmings, clothes and gifts for Luke, his wife, family and the orphanage children.

That led to a not-too-comical comedy of errors: two tires blowing out in a driving rainstorm, the frustration of tracking down a dealer willing to open his store to sell us odd size tires on Christmas day and steering gear trouble, which prayers and a miracle corrected.

We arrived in Guerrero around four o'clock the next morning, soaked, exhausted and with sour dispositions. So that we wouldn't wake up everybody, we stole into the store room, which I had previously cleaned and piled high with blankets and in the dark — we had no lamps or lanterns there — felt for blankets or clothes. There were none. I was more than a little irritated.

All we could do was go to the theater and, wet and shivering, slip into damp sleeping bags to warm up enough to sleep until the sun rose. At daybreak my disposition was not sweetened when I learned that Luke had told the community of Guerrero that we would have Christmas gifts for everybody. We would have needed the logistics of the U.S. Army to take care of the whole village.

"By the way, Luke," I said. "Where are all the blankets and clothes for the children we will soon be taking in?"

He glanced quizzically at me.

"Oh, those? Well, you see, there are so many needy people in Guerrero, we gave them all away — and our food, too!"

It turned out that Luke had taken other unauthorized actions — such as spending all the petty cash and leaving the orphanage children and his family on their own, while he and his wife evangelized in the community.

While we admired his generosity as well as his zeal for spreading the Word, we saw that he was doing what he desired, rather than what he had been called to do and after prayer and serious thought, realized that we would have to replace him. We informed Luke of this and as soon as we could arrange it, Chuck drove him, his wife and family across the border to stay with friends, while Rogelia and I tried to right the ship until we could find the proper director.

For three weeks, I stayed at the orphanage with Rogelia, while Chuck and Andrea ran our North Hollywood household, with friends a telephone call away in the event of an emergency. An emergency occured, but not in North Hollywood.

At twilight two people in an old pickup truck gunned their motors and raced around the building coming dangerously close to a huge pile of heavy lumber nine or ten feet high against the wall of the dormitory, where I stayed with the children.

There seemed to be no point in risking my life and endangering the children by trying to reason with them. I bolted the door and as the children gathered near, I told them, "Don't be afraid. God is watching over us."

Oh, how I wished that there was a phone to call the Delegado! But we were 100 years behind in modern conveniences. I had no car with me and didn't want to risk walking a mile to Guerrero and leaving the children alone.

Off and on, the harassment continued until two in the morning, when we said a final prayer and, in exhaustion, fell asleep. Once I thought I smelled smoke but dismissed the idea and settled into a deeper sleep.

There is no more effective alarm clock than children. Before I had had a chance to get the sand out of my eyes, the little girls rushed in to my bed, shouting in alarm, "Hermana CHAR-la!"

Normally they wouldn't deliberately wake me. All chattering at once, they told me there had been a fire in the lumber pile. My first thought was the smoke I had smelled and then, how could the lumber pile against the wall have been set afire without burning our building down?

Quickly dressing, I went ouside with them and saw something that almost raised goosebumps on my arm. Kerosene soaked rags had been stuffed between the wood pieces and yet the fire had burned only as high as three feet and no wider than that. The burned area was shaped like a fireplace.

There was no way that lumber could have kept from burning all the way through and destroying the building in which we had slept. I lost no time in reporting the event to the portly and excitable Delegado. A reed-thin friend who spent his days loafing in the Delegado's office joined us, pedaling his bicycle as the Delegado and I walked to the orphanage for his investigation.

I showed them the lumber pile fire. The Delegado fell to his knees, feeling the ground underneath. He said to his aide and me, "Seco (dry)." He pulled some of the kerosene soaked rags from between the large pieces of wood. Carefully he studied the fireplace-size burned out part.

"No entiendo," he kept saying. "I do not understand. This building should have burned to the ground. I have never in my life seen anything so strange. No entiendo."

Maybe he didn't understand, but I did. "Señor Delegado, it is a miracle of protection from our wonderful God!" Chuck, a veteran fireman for many years, carried on his own thorough investigation a week later. He agreed that by the laws of physics, the lumber pile and the building should have been ashes. Unlike the Delegado, he understood why they weren't.

The incident left no doubt in our minds. We needed a full-time couple to serve as directors — someone who would be around in case of emergencies and operate the orphanage properly.

One of the last jobs I completed before leaving the orphanage in mid-afternoon was treating some of the children for head lice — small, flat, grey-white organisms which get under the skin or attach themselves to hair follicles and lay eggs.

These children had scratched themselves raw and bloody, so I had to wash their heads carefully and dry them with towels to be boiled later. Then I washed their heads again with Quelle shampoo, which destroys the organisms and their eggs. Before discovering Quelle, we had used kerosene to kill them.

This is an unpleasant job that has to be done, not only for the child with lice but for the protection of others who live with him or her. Lice spread easily and rapidly unless every precaution is taken. When finished, I washed my hands and got ready to return to North Hollywood.

About the time I reached Ensenada, I began scratching my scalp. Then I laughed. "*How suggestible you are!*" Maybe so, but with every passing mile, I found myself itching like fire.

Crossing the border, I soon reached San Ysidro. My head itched so that I could hardly stand it. I stopped at a service station restroom and inspected myself. I saw many patches of raw scalp and was horrified. There was no imagination about it. For the first time in my life, I had lice.

It was around midnight when, on the San Diego Freeway, I saw a sign for a turnoff that up to now had amused me each time I passed it: "Las Pulgas" — the Spanish term for lice.

With my whole scalp on fire, I was in agony all the way to North Hollywood and puzzled about how to treat myself for lice with no drugstore open. Then I remembered we had a big kerosene lamp in the den for use during power outages.

Not wanting to risk spreading lice in the house, I went around to the bedroom window where Chuck was asleep.

"Chuck," I called, finally rousing him. Still more asleep than awake, he couldn't imagine what was happening. "Will you please wake up and bring me the kerosene lamp from the den?"

"Don't bother me about the the kerosene lamp, Charla. Why don't you just turn on the light."

Finally I got through to him, explained my problem and he brought me the lamp. I doused my head and neck, letting it soak for about 10 minutes. Then I went inside and washed it all off with as hot a shower as I could stand.

That cured me of lice, which is synonymous with poverty. I got them off my scalp but if I live to be 100, I will never get them off my mind.

17

DECISION

Probably our eagerness to have permanent directors for the orphanage and build a base for expansion made our committee hire Italian-Americans Willy and Lucinda. On the surface they seemed just right, having had orphanage experience in Ensenada, speaking the language like natives and showing fondness for the children.

When we outlined our orphanage principles and plans, our objectives appeared to be their objectives. After they took charge, I felt confident enough to drive home to take up work with my other family in North Hollywood.

Several weeks later, I brought a load of supplies down to Guerrero and sensed a subtle change in Willy. He was sitting at the kitchen table over a cup of coffee. I poured one for myself, sat opposite him, and asked him for receipts for petty cash expenditures to take back to our committee treasurer.

"What's the matter?" Willy asked with a trace of annoyance. "Don't you trust me?" That troubled me.

"Sure, Willy. If we didn't trust you, we wouldn't have hired you."

"Well?"

"Well, Willy, we need receipts for accurate

orphanage records. We want to be accountable, because our donors have a right to know how their money is being spent."

Willy shrugged. "We've got enough to handle here without saving every scrap of paper."

I looked directly at him.

"Willy," I said, "it may seem like a nuisance to you, but we've got to be businesslike and responsible in all things."

He appeared to be studying the coffee in his cup, glanced up and saw that I wasn't backing down.

"You understand it's nothing personal. The board would expect that from any director here."

"Sure," he mumbled.

The conversation was quite friendly from then on, and I thought we would get the desired cooperation from Willy.

So many important family events took place over several months that I was unable to visit Guerrero, but each month with the delivery of food, Willy would come in contact with a committee member. Once when Dave Taylor delivered the food, he asked for petty cash receipts from Willy, who, with a smirk on his broad, dark-skinned face, asked, "Who gets to see the receipts for the groceries you buy, Dave?"

"The committee," responded Dave, less irritated by Willy's insolence than by his refusal to be questioned and accountable.

Soon Willy resented nearly all direction and suggestions. His insecurity grew. He knew he couldn't work with a group, suspected he might be fired, and feared for the future of "his" orphanage children.

One day on my way through Ensenada, I stopped to see our Mexican attorney.

"Why, Mrs. Pereau, what a surprise," he said.

"It has been quite some time," I agreed.

"No, that is not what I *mean.* I thought you were no longer interested in the orphanage."

Why would he say that?

"I know we've been negligent in not stopping by to see you, but. . .".

"No, Mrs. Pereau, the communication we received was that you and Mr. Taylor were no longer a part of the orphanage committee and your names were taken off the Mexican Corporation."

Now I was upset. *We had just been eased out!*

It was obvious whose behind-the-scenes work had brought this about.

"Neither Dave Taylor nor I ever put in writing to you that our names were to be removed," I replied in as controlled a manner as possible.

"That is true, Mrs. Pereau. I apologize. I should not have taken the action I did on hearsay information. Your names will be restored."

He did the job while I was there.

The time and distance between Ensenada and Colonia Vicente Guerrero cooled me down enough to confront Willy firmly but without anger.

He could sense that something serious had just happened and that it concerned him. I didn't soften my words.

"Willy, I have just come from our corporation attorney in Ensenada."

He became visibly embarrassed.

"I have just had Dave Taylor's and my names restored to the Mexican Corporation, and I'm going to ask you some direct questions."

"That's all I get around here — questions," he replied in a burst of anger. "I'm fed up on them. You can count me out of this place. Once I have another situation, I'll get out of here."

"Is this a resignation?"

"Yeah, that's what it is."

It was a peculiar resignation. He didn't find a new situation. We learned after several weeks that he had acquired ten acres of land near a dry stream bed about a mile away and had already started building his own orphanage. Not being on the scene at all times, we were not immediately aware that he was using some of our building materials and a portable cement mixer that Chuck had given to the orphanage.

The committee was troubled by Willy's action. To build an orphanage so close to ours while staying at our place and using our equipment and supplies seemed unfair.

Eventually Willy moved out and took with him several of our children. Chuck went over to the new orphanage and retrieved the cement mixer and building tools. Willy's logic was that this equipment belonged to him because he now had several of our children.

Soon Willy's orphanage, which appeared to have been built to spite us, developed a bad reputation with case workers. Administration was slipshod. The same failings that had led to his decline with us, led to his downfall. There were no adequate financial books kept, no records on the children and evidence of inadequate care for them. Eventually the Mexican government closed up the orphanage and gave Willy official notice to pack, leave the country and never come back.

Others tried to revive Willy's orphanage. Several directors failed but we could not be critical of their operation. After all, we hadn't won a truckful of blue ribbons in selecting our directors or in the operation of our orphanage.

As we searched for new directors, Chuck and I got

the feeling that perhaps we should volunteer for the position. That would mean that Chuck would have to resign from the fire department before retirement and we would have to dispose of most of our things and sell our home.

One night I had a dream and heard a voice, "Remember Lot's wife." After waking up, I tried to figure out what the dream was trying to tell me and retraced the steps of Lot and his wife. Why did Lot's wife look back? If I had to leave my home, why would I look back? Grandma's handpainted china in the dining room, bone china tea cups in the china cabinet and family pictures on the den wall would be the reasons.

Immediately, I said, *"Lord, would I have to part with these treasures?"* Also, I recognized that God was asking me, *"Lovest thou Me more than these things?"*

Was I willing to follow the Lamb? That morning I went from room to room giving my treasures up to Jesus, willing to part with them all.

Mary Peterson came by and I asked her, "Why did Lot's wife look back?"

"All her friends were there!" she replied.

Mary could break an antique plate and not be bothered but she wouldn't want to lose her friends and church. Chuck's answer was a classic: "She looked back because her husband told her not to."

God had brought me to a place where I was willing to give up all. My values had not been in the right place. After relinquishing everything, I had a great feeling of inner peace and sensed that God was, in fact, not calling us to leave behind our physical things. But He did want to have our willingness.

I still needed confirmation of God's will and wrote to Reverend P. H. P. Gutteridge, a close friend who, when on vacation from the Bible Testimony

Fellowship, would conduct services in our church at the orphanage. I also wrote another precious friend, Jean Darnall in England.

Reverend Gutteridge prayerfully considered my question and replied:

"I do not feel you should live in Mexico. The Lord has others who could do this but *nothing else.* The Lord has given to you the gift of ministering the Word and of inspiring faith and interest in His work. You can do much more good for the orphanage in the States than in Mexico."

Jean Darnall's response was equally emphatic that I continue doing what I was doing and remember an earlier letter in which she had recommended one day a week for fasting and prayer for laborers for His ministry.

Now as I reviewed the confirmations that Chuck and I were not to go to Baja as orphanage directors, we knew we had to fast and pray and that then, the right laborers would come to us. We were given that peace that passes understanding.

One thing the committee agreed upon unanimously: "Never again will we talk someone into coming down to Guerrero. The next couple chosen will have to be called by God into His service."

After fasting and prayer, the answer we got was not the one we expected.

Bill and Kaye Lawrence, a young couple who had visited the orphanage in work parties, attended our board meeting and volunteered. About twenty-eight and the son of a Trenton, Michigan, Presbyterian minister, Bill had married Kaye, a Catholic girl and they had three children. Neither spoke Spanish, and they seemed too young and inexperienced.

"We believe we have been called to the orphanage," Bill said with conviction.

All of us liked the Lawrences but could hardly believe that God had intended them for us. We did our best to discourage them by painting a black picture. It seemed that none of our arguments — the language barrier, their youth and inexperience, and the rigors of living in Guerrero — could discourage them.

At least they scored a big "A" for resistance against solid argument.

"As a young boy in Sunday School, my greatest joy was reading missionary books and I committed my life to the Lord," Bill told us. "More than anything else, I want to be a missionary."

We learned that Bill had impulsively quit the Moody Bible Institute, hoping to join Missionary Aviation Fellowship, then had come to California, married Kaye and had run away from the Lord and all it meant to be a stereotype Presbyterian minister's son. Like his predecessor Jonah, Bill found himself inside a whale of sorts — the cab of an Alpha Beta market truck — training to become a driver. His teacher turned out to be involved in the Navigators program with Bible scriptures plastered all over the walls, so he could memorize out loud for eight hours a day with his captive audience of one at the wheel.

The reason Bill found himself in this situation was godly Presbyterian parents, praying that God would restore their rebellious son. At the end of thirty days, this modern Jonah went home to wife Kaye and told her they had to start back to Christ and attend a Sunday School. Catholic Kaye suggested a compromise church midway between their faiths — the Lutheran St. Olaf's in Garden Grove. Here they met a lovely lady named Ruth Klancke, who led Kaye to a saving knowledge of Christ.

At that point, both Bill and Kaye committed their

lives to the Lord and while visiting the Guerrero orphanage in a work party, realized that supervising an orphanage was to be their life work.

Now as the Lawrences insisted that they should be our new directors, I replied:

"Bill, you and Kaye should understand that the monthly allotment is small," I explained. "Over and above your room and board and incidental expenses, your personal allotment is only $100.00 per month. This token salary is the same for every permanent staff member — scrubwoman or director."

He grinned.

"I guess you don't understand. We're in it for the service — not the money."

That stopped us.

None of the board put it into words, but there were no other candidates for the opening, Bill and Kaye were so dedicated, confident and discouragement-proof that we said:

"All right, go in Jesus' name."

On the way home, Chuck asked, "How long do you think they'll last?"

"Six months," I replied.

"I'll give them three."

The Lord gave them a lot more — over eight years, during which they took the orphanage from infancy to an established work, from a staff of themselves and one to a staff of twenty and launched a building program and an evangelical outreach.

One conclusion I have come to is that the character quality of faithfulness is more important than great talents. Bill and Kaye were faithful.

18

DESIGNED IN HEAVEN

Although appointed by Supreme Headquarters as spearhead of the Baja orphanage in its initial stages, I never forget that a spearhead is not much good without the rest of the spear.

Some parts of that spear came to us in curious ways — especially Harold and Ruth Klancke, Inez Sorenson and Hanne Kristensen Larson and her husband Mark.

When following the guidance of God, I have found it is necessary to keep an open mind in all situations toward all persons. Visiting St. Olaf Lutheran Church, in Garden Grove in 1969, I was introduced by Hal and Barbara Ness to Harold Klancke, a retiree from the federal prison system who was personally responsible for that Church's Mission's Outreach program. Hal said:

"Charla has started an orphanage in Baja California in Colonia Vicente Guerrero."

This large, austere, greying man with a sharp and prominent nose responded in an unexpected way:

"Is it Lutheran?"

"Well, no," I replied, almost apologetically.

"Then why would we be intersted?"

I tried not to be offended by this blunt response

and replied:

"I would like to invite you down. Come see what God is doing with a handful of people."

He nodded assent, and I said to myself, "I'll never see *that* guy again."

Six weeks later, on Thanksgiving weekend, Chuck and I, Mary and Clayton Peterson, a painting contractor, drove down to the orphanage to paint the kitchen. We didn't have enough plastic sheets to cover the whole floor, so while Chuck and Clayton rolled on a fresh, white coat, Mary cooked and I wiped up spatters.

Suddenly my wandering mind snapped to attention when I heard a deep gruff voice say, "Where's a brush?"

The last person in the world I ever expected to see here was Harold Klancke. With him was his wife Ruth, who also wanted to pitch in. As they painted and Clayton learned that Harold was a member of St. Olaf's, he asked, "Isn't your pastor, Reverend Alan Hanson, involved with the charismatics?"

Harold glowered at him and replied, "Yes, there's a bunch of tongue-speakers in our church."

Rather than get involved on this subject, I told myself that I had better retreat but it was already too late. Mary, sweet, beautiful and direct, asked him:

"Oh, don't you speak in tongues?"

Harold stared at her and said, "No."

"That's too bad!" replied Mary.

Meanwhile, Lupita, a precious little raven-haired girl with large brown, soft and loving eyes, came running into the kitchen. Ruth took one look at Lupita, and she took one look at Ruth and it was love at first sight.

With all kinds of informal translators around, Ruth learned from Lupita that she and her older brother, Francisco, had been homeless after her father had killed her mother. Soon Lupita brought in her brother to meet Ruth and Harold Klancke. They learned that Francisco and his best friend Ramiro played guitars and would be performing for services on the next day.

The Klanckes attended Sunday services with us. As I studied Harold's stern, set expression, I wasn't sure it was to his liking but Ruth and the rest of us found great peace in it.

Francisco and Ramiro, who played by ear on several instruments, including the piano, offered an inspired performance on guitars and we were moved as much by the God-given talents of Francisco and Ramiro as by the spoken service. I found myself wishing that these young men could study music in high school — even beyond — and pursue it as a life work.

Later we all sat down to lunch. Harold was opposite me. The first thing he said in his deep dominating voice was:

"Are you one of those?"

I knew what he meant but asked, "One of what?"

"Involved in tongues?"

I looked him squarely in the face and calmly answered, "God has blessed me with a supernatural language of prayer."

"I thought so!" he replied, but his eyes seemed to twinkle.

By then I was beginning to learn that under Harold's forbidding exterior was a heart as soft as butter.

On Harold and Ruth's first visit, Harold's size 13 shoes got covered with Mexican dust, and Ruth's heart had been taken over by Lupita (she even became her financial sponsor) and the Klanckes joined the committee, making frequent trips to Guerrero from Garden Grove.

These faithful servants worked in their 9' by 12' den, converted into an office, forty hours a week for fifteen years, uncompensated. They kept books, paid bills, recorded donations and sent receipts; put together the annual report, carried on correspondence for sponsorship programs and bought groceries and transported them. Harold and Ruth put sound business procedure into the function of treasurer and secretary.

Rounding a curve in a remote area, the white panel truck in which they were transporting a ton of groceries and provisions to the orphanage went out of control and rolled over. Their cargo catapulted from side to side, scattering food, paint and cleaning products along the road in the dry, rocky terrain where the accident occurred. Immediately, people came from nowhere to their assistance. Miraculously, Ruth and Harold sustained only minor injuries. Passers-by salvaged almost all the monthly supplies and carried them to the orphanage. The insurance company replaced the totaled van and an anonymous agent picked up the deductible.

Unable to make the next trip with her husband, Ruth called and said, "Charla, I'm so afraid to have Harold make that long trip by himself. You know how independent he is, he will never let anyone else drive and he won't ask for help. Besides, please don't tell anyone but I think he nodded off just before we hit that awful curve. Could you call and ask if you could ride along?"

I assured her that I would be glad to and would make him think he was doing me a favor. I waited a few minutes and called Harold. "Can I hitch a ride with you to Guerrero on the grocery run?" I asked.

"I'm a little short of gas money." He answered in his usual direct manner. "Okay," he said, "but I don't want you talking all the way and get down here early, 6 a.m. not 6:10!"

At 6:07 we waved goodbye to Ruth, asked God for travelling mercies and then I very discreetly offered to drive should he get tired. Ten minutes later Harold pulled over to the right hand curb at the entrance to the Garden Grove freeway. He got out of the car, walked around to the other side, opened the door and said, "You can take it from here." (A major concession for Harold.) As I drove, Harold shared stories of his encounters as a prison guard with such famous characters as the Birdman of Alcatraz and Max Factor.

Nine hours later, with Colonia Guerrero in sight, he told me to pull over. "I'll take it from here," he said.

What a welcome Harold received as he stepped out of the van from the driver's seat. A throng of children joyuously exclaimed "Klancke! Klancke!" as they looked for a big hug, some goodies or a pat on the head from "Grandpa Klancke", their patriarch.

My eyes filled with tears and an exhortation came to my mind, *"Take from no man his dignity."* This was to be Harold's and my "modus operandi" for the next two years.

Eventually Harold became a marvelous advocate for his pastor, Reverend Hanson and for those others who had received the baptism in the Holy Spirit. I shall never stop thanking God for the Klanckes and their unstinting contributions to the orphanage.

As desperately as we needed the Klanckes, so did we require a gifted teacher to instruct children of the American staff. The answer to our prayers was named Inez Sorenson. It wasn't easy for optimistic, confident Inez Sorenson to retire after thirty-three years in the Santa Maria public school system. She felt a stirring to go into God's work and had this confirmed by a prophecy that "God was calling her to full-time missionary service."

She prayed, "Lord, my heart's desire is to go anywhere in the world for you but please don't take me where it's hot. If possible, I would prefer to be near my grandchildren."

A friend invited her to attend a conference on missions held by the Wycliffe organization, translators of the Bible into a multitude of languages. Inez volunteered to teach children of missionaries.

Wycliffe recognized Inez' excellent qualifications and in view of her good health, optimism and enthusiasm, thought she could make valuable contributions in Papua, New Guinea.

Papua, New Guinea! Inez visualized the steamy heat of this South Pacific land along the equator and her optimism plummeted. After a few tears she turned to Jesus, saying, "I will go there if you want me to but not by choice."

Inez sold her home and most of her possessions and stored what was left in a 25-foot trailer. She waited for orders from Wycliffe. Then, on her last screening, she was found to have met all qualifications but one and was turned down.

The Wycliffe executive who notified her got a sudden inspiration and, from his Huntington Beach office, phoned Dave Taylor in nearby Costa Mesa.

"Say, Dave," he said. "We have a fantastic retired teacher whom we can't use. Can you use her at the orphanage?"

"Can we?" shouted Dave. "We've been praying for a person like that!" In a matter of minutes, Dave had Inez on long-distance phone, telling her that she was

desperately needed at the orphanage.

"What's the climate like in Guerrero?" Inez asked.

"About the same as in Santa Maria," Dave responded.

That cinched it. Inez would definitely come to Guerrero. Wycliffe's loss was our gain. Inez had been told about the rough, narrow, seemingly non-existent roads and hairpin mountain turns — real hazards to a 25-foot trailer — but nothing daunted this gutsy grandma of sixty-eight.

She said goodbye to family and friends and set out on the most adventurous trip of her life. In Tijuana she had the adrenalin-pumping experience of accidentally driving the wrong direction on a one-way street. God protected her from everything except a $17 traffic ticket.

Inez tutored in all grades from the first to high school, along with Sonya Bertelsen who had to return to Phoenix. But Inez does much more than teach. She loves the children and substitutes for the Grandma they all wish they had. Any of them who loses a button knows where to find Grandma Inez, who quickly sews it on. She fixes everything for her children — bruised knees to broken hearts.

One of the boys needed a suit for his eighth grade graduation. Inez took on the assignment, although she had no pattern and couldn't buy one anywhere in Baja. Kaye, on her way to Tijuana, crossed the border, guessed the boy's size and bought a pattern for Inez.

The fabric she had to work with was not the most durable and if she made many mistakes would probably have been ruined. She made the suit, and it came out well, fitting the boy perfectly.

Inez thanked God, marveling how he had prepared her for this work.

"Several years ago, just for fun, I made my husband two suits," she says. "It took two weeks of measuring, sewing, ripping out, remeasuring and sewing again. If the material hadn't been strong, it would have worn out long before the suits were finished to a perfect fit. The Lord knew I would need that experience in Baja. He knew I would not have that same quality fabric or that length of time to make this suit."

Just as Inez came to us as a gift from God, so did Hanne Kristensen Larson. A tall and beautiful Danish farm girl who worked her way through high school and college. She has a master's degree in education and home economics and speaks five languages fluently, including Spanish and English. Hanne, in a group of five, attended a teachers' retreat in Spain. There she had a renewal in the Lord and prayed to be used in a unique way to reach the lost for Christ.

Joining Youth With A Mission in Lausanne, Switzerland, she attended the Munich Olympic Games as part of an evangelical outreach team. After the cold-blooded murder of the Israeli athletes, this team and other dedicated young people, went on a candlelight procession as a memorial to the dead.

Back in Lausanne, she received a prophecy, "One day soon you will be serving the Lord in a Mexican orphanage." Immediately after this, a leader of Youth With A Mission came to her with a confirming scripture (Haggai 2:10): "On the 24th of the 9th month of the second year of Darius, the Word of the Lord came to the prophet Haggai."

She prayed and meditated on these words, knowing that some year on that date she would be taken to the prophesied place of service. Returning to Denmark, she taught for a while and, from an unexpected source, received money for a one-way ticket to Southern California, where she stayed with a girl she had met in Munich, Marjorie Deal of Pacoima.

Often she fasted and prayed, asking, "God, when are you going to use me in Mexico?" Two weeks later, after attending a service at Osborne Neighborhood Church, she met a young man who, out of a clear sky said, "Oh, you're the girl from Denmark. I understand you're interested in work at an orphanage in Mexico."

Hanne was amazed. The fellow took a scrap of paper from his wallet, scribbled a phone number on it and said, "Call Charla Pereau. She's connected with an orphanage in Baja, California."

On the next morning, Hanne and I were talking over cups of coffee in my kitchen. I was overwhelmed with this girl who wanted a humble job in a Mexican orphanage. This rare jewel had a graduate degree, fluency in five languages — while some of us have trouble with one — had worked in various countries and even had helped establish a Sunday school in Spain.

I got on the phone and poured the good news into Harold Klancke's ear.

"Charla, that's great, but we don't have enough money to support the present staff."

I repeated the qualifications of Hanne, and he said, "Charla, we don't have the money!"

Feeling a powerful move of the Holy Spirit, I knew Hanne represented the sovereign will of God for the orphanage. I phoned Dave Taylor, who always has faith for God's provision of financial support. When finances are low and the need is great, I say, "Lord, be it done according to Dave's faith." He heard the story and suggested, "Why not invite

Hanne to spend two weeks at the orphanage, talk to Bill and Kaye Lawrence, learn all about it, and pray. We can't give her any promises beyond that."

It was on Sunday, September 23, when I telephoned Hanne to explain the arrangement. "I'm attending a wedding tonight, but I'll drive you to Guerrero on Monday."

Hanne cried out, "That's the *24th day of the ninth month!"*

I couldn't understand her excitement. After all, September 24th wanders around every year.

"Hanne, let me repeat. This is just for two weeks."

"I understand, Charla, but I want you to know I won't be coming back in two weeks. Guerrero is the place that God wants me to be!"

Did I have some kind of nut on the other end of the line? Sensing my reaction, Hanne quickly told me her prophecy and then I couldn't wait to deliver her to her destination.

Hanne proved to be right. She stayed for three years, not two weeks. Finances came in to support her. This loving servant of God blended in beautifully with the staff and children. She taught flawless Spanish and became so invaluable that she was given an additional duty as housemother to the girls. All the fruits of the Spirit seemed manifested in our Danish Delight.

Shortly before Hanne's arrival, a disillusioned young man, Mark Larson, came to the orphanage to find himself. He found even more. The gardener had just left, so Mark took that job.

Through working close to God's earth — tilling, planting, watering and weeding — he rediscovered his lost faith and rededicated himself to the Lord.

All of us were happy to see a warm friendship

growing between Hanne and Mark. On a glorious Easter Sunday morning at breakfast they were sitting in their usual places across from one another. Hanne said something and her eyes and Mark's locked.

"You know, Hanne," Mark said. "You're a girl and I'm a boy," and there was one of those inner knowings.

A few weeks later they announced their intentions to be married in the fall. At that time, they took a leave and flew to Denmark to be with Hanne's parents. Not long after they were married, Hanne began experiencing blackouts and stammering speech. A medical examination revealed a result that devastated her, Mark and her parents — a tumor which would require surgery. Hanne and Mark took the case to Jesus in prayer. Admitted to the hospital for the agonizing final tests before scheduled brain surgery, Hanne was visited by a group of Christians, who laid hands on her and prayed. Mark had phoned Ruth Klancke, known for her intercessory prayer ministry, and the orphanage board also prayed.

Tests came back and the results mystified doctors. The tumor which had been unquestionably visible in X-rays had vanished. While Hanne went back to teaching, Mark attended Bible school in Denmark and they seemed to be happy. As much as we missed them we were not sure they would return to Colonia Vicente Guerrero.

Dave and Audrey Taylor

Harold and Ruth Klancke

Ann Mills

Inez Sorenson

Pedro

Lucio

Mary Peterson

Jean and Elmer Darnall

Lu Ann White, Secretary

Max & Alicia Christian Administrators

Maynard Jones & Ralph Bingham Help to transport supplies

Javier, one of our orphans, and Abrahana Arce, houseparents

Juan and Elisa Carrillo
Tijuana students

Our pastoral staff

OUR STAFF

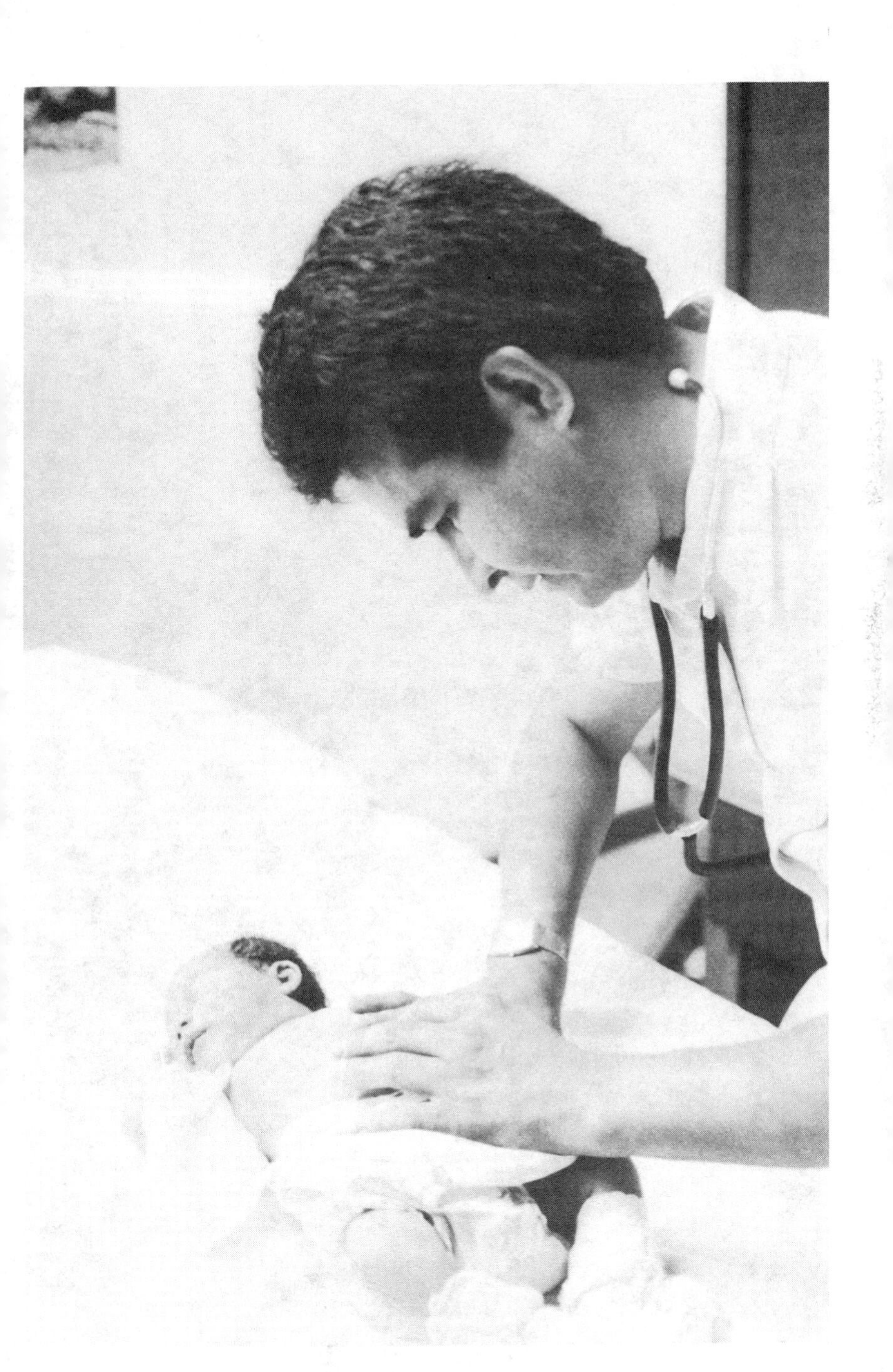

THE CLINIC

ELISA AND ALICIA

19

STRANGE AND WONDERFUL THINGS

Occasionally, during our on-the-job training in orphanage management, we made a few mistakes and God, in His infinite tenderness, love and mercy, took our good intentions and unintentional blunders and molded them into something beautiful.

One of His many miracles of compensation still shines brightly in my memory. When our original five-couple committee took over the orphanage, we saw our ministry solely as fulfilling the body, mind and spiritual needs of homeless Mexican children. Soon we had that limited view shattered.

People of all ages in Southern California — particularly the young — heard about our work through churches and began coming to Guerrero for weekends, a month or even a summer vacation to wash windows, scrub walls, paint, pour concrete, build chicken coops and animal enclosures, roll socks and rock babies.

Surprisingly, our staff of Mexican and American workers had quite a spiritual impact on them. When our visiting helpers saw these dedicated, unstinting individuals cheerfully working from sunup to sundown for just $100 a month and board and room — living sacrifices to the Lord Jesus — they found new purpose for their lives. Some received Christ and others committed themselves unconditionally to the Lord.

All seemed to have caught a revelation as to how a life could be used and changed in serving the King of Kings. The example of Christ inside our staff showing on the outside drove home to me the truth of Oliver Goldsmith's statement that "we preach a better sermon with our lives than with our lips."

We came to another realization, through a certain happening, that we had an obligation to plan ahead and be fully prepared for volunteers with specific work projects and all materials required on hand as well as adequate food and housing.

During Easter week a young people's group from Emmanuel Lutheran Church in North Hollywood, made reservations to come to Guerrero and help us with the work. Our dear friends, Ken and Bev Liskum, were their leaders. Somehow there was a breakdown in communications between the man who coordinates such arrangements and the committeeman who orders material and food for work parties.

It was late at night when the Liskums, their party of 30 and Chuck and I pulled into the orphanage. We were greeted by Bill Lawrence, who asked, "Where's the barbed wire?"

"What barbed wire?" I asked.

"The wire to fence in the 72 acres," replied Bill. "That's why this party is here."

The Liskums, Chuck and I, groaned in unison.

Now we had 30 charged-up, enthusiastic young people all set to go and no work project for them. *What were we going to do?* On top of that, we had 30 more voracious appetites and our pantry was nearly empty.

We didn't want to throw ice water on the hopes of these kids, so I breathed a silent prayer. "Lord, we need barbed wire and a loaves-and-fishes miracle."

Fortunately there was enough food for a few meals and work was not supposed to start until the next morning. Before the youth group was awake, we all met at the 5:30 A.M. staff meeting around a table in the dining room. Since the start, our orphanage staff began each day with prayers and thanksgiving and meditating on God's Word. This, to me, is the key to success of the orphanage ministry. We prayed for guidance, for the children and for strength and wisdom for the day's tasks. The cook, Kathy Griffin, asked prayer for more food in her pantry. "With our visitors, we don't have enough even to finish the day," she informed us.

"Here's an idea," I said. "Kids spend money like water nowadays. Let's just level with them. At breakfast let's just tell them there's been a breakdown in communications and about the food situation and pass the hat, take the money to Ensenada and buy food.

Hanne, our beautiful teacher from Denmark, smiled: "Charla, we've never violated our principle of only letting God know of our needs and trusting Him for provision. We really should lay this need on the table before God. It is then His responsibility to provide."

How could I do anything but agree, because this had been my lofty theory from the beginning? When we prayed, I also prayed with thanks and praise to God for always bringing the someone who buoys up my faith when it is sinking. With our usual closing, we joined hands and, in Spanish and English, we said, "Have a blessed day."

As we rose from the table, I wondered, "*God, how are you going to employ these willing but idle hands and how are you going to feed these young people?*"

One of the answers came almost instantly from Chuck.

"These kids don't even know they were supposed to be fencing the acreage. They don't really care what they will be doing as long as they are doing. We need a lot of sidewalks to keep dirt from being tracked inside."

Everyone agreed and that made Chuck happy, because he enjoys concrete work and would have the fun of showing the young people how to do it. Bill Lawrence said, "Great idea, Chuck. We can buy all the cement we need at San Vicente, and the kids can haul sand and rocks from the wash. Loading and bringing sand and rock should keep more of them busy."

"Is there enough petty cash to buy cement?" Chuck asked.

"Well . . ."replied Bill. He didn't have to say any more. Chuck whipped out his wallet, and I dug into my purse. We looked up at Bill at the same time. Neither of us had more than a few dollars.

Much later, just after we got up from the breakfast table — about 9:00 o'clock — a beautiful motor home, so long that I wondered how it had negotiated the hair-pin turns enroute, stopped on the grounds. Out came a smiling, middle-aged couple.

"We saw a sign on the main road about your home for needy children," the woman told us, as Chuck and I and some of the children gathered around. "My husband remembered that a woman had spoken to a deacon's meeting at the Bel Air Presbyterian Church about this work."

"May we look around?" asked the man.

We escorted them around the various buildings and as they walked through the kitchen, the man spotted a little wooden box marked "Love Gifts." he took something out of his billfold and dropped it through the slot. They wished us well, said goodbye, entered their motor home and started down the dusty road. We were dying to know what he had put into the Love Gift box. Bill Lawrence opened it up, and there was a gorgeous green $100 bill, more than enough to buy cement and keep the teen-agers busy.

All through the day a strong wind blew but our volunteer work team kept cheerfully at their jobs. In the afternoon, the wind became a violent gale, blasting sand and dust through the orphanage area.

Yet the wild wind was not the major problem. We were still concerned with how God was going to feed our visitors.

Early that evening a bright yellow and black trimmed bus full of Boy Scouts from Hawthorne, California, pulled up in front of the orphanage. Out of the bus jumped the adult leader of the group, as uniformed boys peered out through all the windows.

"I'm Reverend Sherman Korshaven," he said, as we introduced ourselves. "We were down at the Bay of Concepcion for an Easter vacation camping trip. A tremendous wind came up in the night and blew down some of our tents. This morning and into the afternoon the winds were so violent that we took a vote and unanimously decided to go back home.

"As the bus traveled north on Highway #1, the scouts saw the sign, "Home for Needy Children," and said, "It's ridiculous to carry all of this food back home. Let's leave it at the orphanage."

Bill and Kaye, the Liskims and Chuck and I glanced at each other in amazement and joy.

When the Reverend Korshaven saw the looks on

our faces, he asked, "You *can* use some food, can't you?"

"Yes, we *can!*" I answered. Our eyes bulged as the scouts unloaded all kinds of food: hash, pork and beans, soup, huge cans of vegetables and fruit, fruit juices, large sacks of rice and beans and cases of powdered Carnation milk.

How we thanked God and His good scouts.

Our pantry runneth over!

With due credit to our directors and regular staff, I don't know how we could have gotten the job done without volunteer help from all quarters, mainly church groups. The things to be done seemed endless — walls to be washed or painted, gardens to be weeded, mountains of mending waiting for menders, roofs to be tarred — and then it's time to start all over again.

Usually youth groups pitch in and turn the work into fun and feelings of accomplishment for a worthy cause. But I can't forget one particular work session that almost ended in tragedy. On a Thanksgiving weekend, a group of teenagers from Central Lutheran Church in Van Nuys, including our daughter Andrea, Diana and Barbara Peterson, Liz Gjelten (daughter of the pastor) and the two Perner boys, rented a truck driven by Dave Anderson, the youth director, and arrived safely at the orphanage.

Mary Peterson, Juliana Perner and I drove down together to help in food preparation and serving of the visitors and any other jobs that had to be done.

On Sunday morning after breakfast, with their work accomplished, the group piled into the back of the canvas-covered truck, in high spirits despite rain that began to fall, and headed toward the main road.

Mary, Juliana and I remained behind to mop up

and put the place back in shape. By early afternoon we started homeward. After the ordeal of driving the worst part of the trip I stopped, as usual, at a Pemex station in Ensenada for a break and fuel.

One of the attendants whom I knew, a swarthy, brown-mustached young man, nodded to me.

"Oh, you — the American lady." His English was a bit broken, but not enough so that I couldn't put it back together again. "Do you know of the . . . how is it said?" And when he couldn't think of the word, he crashed his hands together.

My blood almost froze. Did he mean there had been a crash?

"Was there an accident?"

"Si . . . *accident*" he replied, "un trucke grande near Santo Tomas . . . American truck . . . jovenes (young people)." Now my heart was racing and how agonizing it was, with the langauage barrier, to extract the facts. But this was the story that emerged.

The American truck had skidded into a truck driven by a Mexican. Someone had been seriously injured — perhaps killed. The service station attendant wondered if this party had something to do with me, "The American lady."

The more I thought about Andrea, Diana, Barbara, Liz Gjelten, the Perner boys and the others in the work party, the more I became concerned about their welfare and about the ramifications from the complexities of an accident in Mexico.

"Where can I get more information?" I asked the attendant. He raised up the palm of his hand for me to wait and ran over to his boss inside. I saw him talk animatedly and then gesture in our direction. He rushed back,"I go with you to police," he said, and we scrambled into the car, following his directions.

He interpreted for us, and we learned that the

description of the truck tallied with that of the church group's rented vehicle. One of the policemen who spoke English then came over and I asked him:

"Was the driver of the American truck held?"

"No, the damaged truck was impounded, but he was released — this youth worker from the American church — and allowed to look after those in his charge."

I breathed a deep sigh of relief. Dave's release, in itself, was a miracle in Mexico.

"Were any of the young people injured?"

"Yes," he replied, "but I do not know how badly."

Then he explained that Dave Anderson had flagged rides for his group at the scene of the accident. I knew the San Tomas area. The traffic was light. Sometimes it would be an hour before a northbound car would pass but the officer said that Dave was able to arrange rides for everyone in the party within minutes. Another miracle!

"The young man will return to Ensenada tomorrow to make a full report," continued the officer.

"Where were the injured taken?" I asked.

"The Americans? Probably San Diego. The Mexican driver of the other truck was taken to the Ensenada hospital. When the American truck crashed into the other, this man, with his ten children in the cab and on the back of the truck, was critically injured. His children were not scratched but he is not expected to live."

Picturing the father of ten on his deathbed and the possible plight of his wife and large family, I felt a sense of great grief and responsibility. Another part of me was in the U.S., wondering whether Andrea was among those injured. I thought of her earlier handicap, the ear problems, and how Jesus, the Healer, helped her over that and other rough places and I again committed her to the arms of the Great Physician.

"How I would like to visit the man in the Ensenada hospital!" I said, and my friend, the service station attendant, nodded vigorously, "Senora, I take you."

The hospital was near the Pemex station, where we dropped off our guide with thanks. I was grateful that Juliana Perner could speak Spanish well and we could communicate.

As soon as Juliana, Mary and I entered the hospital, I felt a letdown. No one was at the reception desk to give us information, and not a nurse was visible in the corridor. We wandered helplessly down a hallway, opened a door, and were surprised to see white-garbed, masked surgeons performing an operation. Quickly we closed the door and continued toward the end of the corridor, where a group of downcast people stood waiting.

Could this be the injured man's family?

Juliana inquired, and it was.

"The father is in the hospital room in a coma. He hasn't been conscious since he was removed from the scene of the accident," she told us.

"Juliana, will you please ask if they mind if we go in the room and pray for the man? Tell them we often pray for the sick."

She did, and they approved. In this grave hour, they would welcome such help — even from Americans.

Mary and I tiptoed inside the private room, one of us on each side of the bed, while Juliana stood at the foot. Seeing the man gave us a shock. His head was extensively bandaged. What was exposed of his face was so swollen that the areas of his closed eyes were like slits. His brown skin had a ghostly pallor. We could not even tell if he was breathing. The heavy stillness of death hung over the room.

"Let's pray," I said. Mary took one of his hands and I the other, while Juliana remained where she was and prayed.

"Jesus, touch this man," I said. "Let your life flow through this broken body and make it whole."

At the same time, it seemed that the man's eyelids were moving ever so slightly. Then, slowly, his eyes opened as far as the swelling would permit. We knew instantly that he knew we were praying for him. He tried to speak and at first, nothing came out. Again he tried.

"Dios . . . la bendiga." (God bless you), he said in gratitude.

And we knew that the healing virtue of Jesus had flowed through him and was mending him now.

Singing praises, Mary, Juliana and I left. Juliana told the anxious group in the corridor that Jesus had delivered His healing power and that the man was conscious.

Eagerly and quickly we returned to the road. When we reached home we learned that only Liz Gjelten had been injured badly enough to need hospitalization. She was in San Diego with a severe whiplash. Andrea got only a good jarring. Diane and Barbara Peterson and the Perner boys were all fine.

Later we learned that the Mexican truck driver had recovered fully.

20

GREG

Sticky problems were so much a part of operating the orphanage that I often asked God to keep life at home simple and easy to handle.

Sometimes He did.

I certainly wasn't looking for added family responsibility on that June morning in 1972 when Evelyn Paulson, the parish worker at Emmanuel Lutheran Church, phoned me. She had just visited a family which was no longer attending church and had learned of a strange situation there.

"Charla, a homeless fifteen-year-old boy named Greg who was born in Mexico is staying with this family. They are giving him only very temporary sanctuary. The boy seems to be entangled in a hopeless maze of litigation and in constant fear of deportation."

I felt an instant pang of sympathy but didn't see how we could help. Evelyn continued talking:

"Greg is a fine boy, but what a tough life he has had." And she poured out the details. Greg was a prostitute's son from the streets of Mexicali — one of many children. An uncle who liked Greg and saw a spark of potential even in a seven-year-old had heard of a wealthy widow in one of the San Fernando

Valley's most fashionable communities who was willing to adopt a homeless Mexican boy.

The uncle secured a tourist's card and brought this child across the border. The woman was delighted with Greg. Somehow, through a quirk in official procedure, she had legally adopted him without having secured the proper immigration paper. She taught him English, bought him quality clothing, enrolled him in the best of schools, and impressed upon him her burning ambition for him to become a concert pianist.

An intelligent boy, Greg learned English quickly and well, becoming completely Americanized.

Through the years he learned to play the piano and worked hard to satisfy his new mother by practicing for hours every day.

But part of the Americanizing process was playing baseball and other games which he preferred, to playing piano. Greg knew he was not cut out to be a concert artist and objected to being her little Lord Fauntleroy.

Originally, the widow was enamored with motherhood; but when her cute, little "puppy" turned into a real person, a boy with hopes, dreams and desires which were different than her own, she became irritated, then by degrees, angry. She contacted his uncle in Mexico and they devised a plot to have him kidnapped and taken back to Mexico. But the plan was foiled.

When he was fifteen, their smoldering conflict burst into flames. Two strong wills clashed.

Embarrassed by her inability to cope with Greg and infuriated with his oppositon, she reported to immigration authorities that he was an illegal alien. Greg was surprised about this and stunned when he was deported to Mexico along with an airplane load of individuals who had crossed the border without proper papers.

By this time, he could no longer speak Spanish, knew no one in Mexico and for a time, became utterly demoralized in this unfamiliar environment. Then, resourcefully, he made his way back to the border.

Taken for an American-born Mexican — his English was flawless — he had no problems crossing over and getting back to the San Fernando Valley home of a school friend.

"Charla," Evelyn said, "Greg's adoptive mother is still intent on having him deported. He has no family in Mexico. He is a promising young man. Would you and Chuck consider taking him in?"

Although deeply touched with the story of Greg, I replied, "We have our hands full. Craig is sixteen. Dana is seventeen, and this work in Mexico gives us much more than we can handle."

"I'm sure that's true, Charla, but Greg is such a *nice* young man. Will you at least help him? You know quite a bit about immigration with all your goings back and forth across the border. Please advise him on how to get straightened out with immigration."

"All right Evelyn. Send him over but don't you dare give him any idea that we would consider taking him in!"

"Of course not," she assured me.

As I greeted Greg at the front door, I liked him. He was tall, thin and had beautiful curly dark brown hair and surprisingly white teeth. What drew me to him most was the sadness of a thousand hurts in his large brown eyes.

Chuck, who was at home that day, warmly welcomed Greg into the house and we all sat at the table in our sunny kitchen. Quickly, unemotionally he told us his life story, almost identical to Evelyn's account.

My sympathy was stirred more by Greg himself than by what he said — the fact that he was a little round-shouldered, somewhat "hang-dog" and that his large, sensitive brown eyes were filled with rejection, hurt and fear. A question flashed into my mind and I asked:

"Greg, have you ever loved anybody?"

"No," he replied slowly.

"Has anybody ever loved you, Greg?"

For a fraction of a second he hesitated, then said, "I don't think so, Mrs. Pereau."

His directness and complete honesty gave me a strong feeling: *This young man needs to be salvaged!*

Then I glanced at Chuck to note his reaction and instantly saw in his eyes that it was the same as mine. I told Greg briefly about our family and Chuck then took over:

"Greg, all of us attend church and Sunday School. This goes for relatives or anybody who lives with us. We have rigid standards — no drinking, smoking or swearing. Everybody is at the evening meal at six o'clock, where we read the Word and pray together."

"If you think you could fit into this strict lifestyle, we will invite you to make your home with us." Chuck didn't even glance in my direction.

"Mr. Pereau, I have no idea what Christianity is, but I'm sure I will have no problem in conforming to your life."

That was how Greg became a member of the family. We moved him in the boy's back bedroom. Dana soon left to be on his own and Greg shared a room with Craig and Charles Curtis. Late at night Greg became more communicative. He would sit at the kitchen table or come and sit on our bed and ask perplexing questions. "Why do the innocent suffer? Are there absolutes and who set them? Do you really believe the inerrancy of scripture? Why don't you play poker? Why are you concerned about Mexico?"

On one such evening Greg asked, "Do you really believe in the virgin birth of Jesus?" I answered, "Greg, what are you going to do with this man Jesus? Are you going to reject Him because you can't understand Him or the truth intellectually? You have made your intellect God. I can answer some of your questions and you can learn all about Jesus, know all about Him but never really know Him. Are you, Greg, going to be the master of your fate or are you going to let Jesus be your master by faith?"

That night at the kitchen table at 6202 Radford, North Hollywood, Greg confessed unbelief as sin, asked God to forgive him and to help him learn to love and accept Jesus as his master and friend. He wrote his adoptive mother and asked her forgiveness for the hurts he had caused her and told her he had become a true born again Christian.

Greg, who had refused to play the piano, began playing after the family had gone to bed. Chuck and I laid in bed many nights blessing and thanking God for Mozart and Beethoven piano concertos.

It took several years for the rejection, hurt and fear to leave Greg's eyes, for him to accept and give love.

Greg became an outstanding scholar in high school and beyond. He was graduated Cum Laude from Oral Roberts University.

When he walked across the platform at Oral Roberts University during commencement exercises, I thrilled to see him decorated with an extra gold cord for his high honor. The thought came to me.

"Here is our Greg: from the streets of Mexicali to the halls of ORU. What a long way he has come!" I wept for joy.

GREG

21

THE PAIN OF LOSING

It would be an exaggeration to say that all children in the orphanage turned out well. We have failures — painful failures. Older children and youths sometimes cannot or will not break the grip of strong conditioning on their lives.

We don't hand-pick children who are most likely to succeed. We take them as they come. Most of them have been abandoned or orphaned. A small percentage come right off the streets of Ensenada and Tijuana — those caught stealing or vandalizing property. In Mexican criminal justice, there are no such things as wrist-slappings and Juvenile Hall for such offenses. These children are thrown in jail among hardened criminals and subjected to brutality and the abominations of prisons, including perversions.

Among men about to be transported to a Mexicali prison was Pedro, a small and wiry boy of 12. Pedro was a notorious thief. The social worker, foreseeing that evil influences of prison could only corrupt the boy more, pulled him out of the line and recommended to the police officer in charge, "Let's send him down to Guerrero. Maybe they can do something with him."

The policeman agreed, and that's how we got Pedro, unbelievably strong, tough and belligerent for his small size. He reminded me of a dog or cat that had been in many scraps, dark brown eyes darting back and forth, alert for threats from any side, dark skin and prominent ears poking out from thick, brown, unkempt hair. His small, surly face seemed to contain a thunderstorm ready to happen.

With his fists, Pedro let everyone, large and small, know that nobody was going to get in his way. Many times in the beginning, we had to pull him off various boys and reprimand him.

"Look, Pedro," I told him. "We have no fighting in this place. This is a home where love rules."

He looked at me in bewilderment. Strength, not love, ruled in the streets where he had lived.

Pedro, crackling with electric energy and hyperactive, always seemed caged in the boy's dormitory and in the dining room. Even our 72 acres were the equivalent of a cage to this boy, who had free run on the streets of Ensenada.

Eating three meals a day puzzled him. On the streets he had been accustomed to eating and drinking only when hungry or thirsty. One of the rules we had was that children were not allowed to take food from the kitchen or dining room. So what did Pedro do but eat what he wanted, sneak out the rest and stash it away, just in case there wasn't anything for tomorrow.

School was nonsense to Pedro. He was a non-stop fidgeter and squirmer, driven to escape the classroom as soon as he was inside. He couldn't hold still for study that had nothing to do with his survival or subjects that seemed unimportant.

Eventually he learned to tolerate and even enjoy some of the kids but he was programmed to be a loner. He loved a few of the older people and occasionally he would respond to them. I'll never forget the first time I hugged him. He had never known affection and didn't know how to receive or give it. He became rigid. It seemed as if I were embracing a railroad tie. After a half year or so, he was better able to put up with it. Eventually, there were times when I felt he even enjoyed a hug but was never free of embarrassment.

Pedro quickly grasped the fact that there was status in having relatives who cared, in having roots — rather than being a tumbleweed. He noted the joy in the eyes of a child who received a postcard, letter, or visit from a parent or grandparent and the envy and longing in eyes of those who witnessed this. So Pedro created his own status with swollen stories about his wealthy parents that everybody listened to with fascination but nobody believed.

My happiest time with Pedro was the day when he received Jesus Christ as his personal Saviour. His brown eyes, which had been dull, almost ignited with a new light. We were all thankful that he stopped running off for days at a time and stealing. Soon he was singing happily, particularly one song, "Lord, send us rain, Lord send us rain . . .".

One bright, sunny morning, during a break from loading wheelbarrows full of rock for use as a base for concrete, Pedro and I spotted a small brown sparrow singing a cheerful song in a dusty pine near the front of the little flat-roofed church.

Impulsively, I called out, "Good morning, bird. How are you today?"

Pedro shook his head at me as if I had lost my mind.

"That bird doesn't understand English," he said with disdain.

"What language does he speak?" I asked.

"Spanish!"

"All right, Pedro, but he understands English."

Pedro snorted. "Maybe so, but he doesn't like it."

For a period, Pedro swung like a pendulum between his new life as a Christian and the old life. He would run away, steal, pummel one of the kids, or tell a lie and then repent and feel obvious sorrow for his misdeeds.

Finally, after two years, Pedro threw his belongings into a brown paper bag one night and disappeared. We never heard from him again. An ending like this makes sadness cut into my heart.

Of course, there were Pedros with other names who followed a similar pattern — little street boys whom we had the privilege of serving for only a short time, building their malnourished, rib-showing bodies, delousing them, offering friendship, love and the teachings of Jesus.

Some of the teachings rolled off, some stuck, but basically, they could not feel comfortable because they had had no experience living in a family or sharing, adjusting and conforming. Fantastic at picking locks, stealing and escaping (nothing was sacred to them) they would just take off.

Pancho was one of them. In the night, he would pick a lock, find a shoeshine kit, and be gone. Several times he came back for short periods but then, just as he seemed to be adjusting, he would disappear in the dark of night. Often as we drove through Ensenada and Tijuana, I would see the Pedros and Panchos roving like a pack of dogs, sleeping under bridges, in washes, doorways, even on the dumps.

This always gave me a new charge of determination and strength to try to do better. If we had failed with several, we could pray and work harder, wiser and with more patience. With God's help we would win!

Another kind of disappointment that cuts like a razor is losing children to one or both parents entitled to them but unable to bring them up properly or to provide them with a wholesome environment.

To know most of these youngsters is to love them. I shall never forget four little girls, daughters of an alcoholic prostitute, who had been brought to us from the streets of Tijuana. These children had learned to beg for money to support their mother when her earnings were low.

All of the children were precious in their god-given individual ways — especially five-year-old Marta, a sweet and bubbly little child with a round face, black hair and olive-shaped, sparkling black eyes. She was socially adaptable, able to play in harmony with others or happily by herself.

Several months later, their mother came to the orphanage for her children. It almost broke my heart. *I would probably never again see Marta.* Even worse was the thought that she and her sisters would be living in a one room hut in Ensenada, where their mother practiced her trade.

Much to my surprise, the mother gave us her new address. On some of my trips through Ensenada to Guerrero, I would stop to see the children, now barefoot and dirty with hair uncombed and unwashed and bring them a box of goodies.

One day Chuck and I parked in front of the hut and little Marta came running to us, jumping up and down in excitement. We bent over and she eagerly tried to encircle us both in a hug with her short, chubby arms.

Marta was the only one at home. As I removed a

box of food from the back of the station wagon and brought it into the hovel, the little girl looked up at me with joy and gratitude. Never in my life have I been thanked so well without words. For her age, Marta had incredible social sense. She wanted to give as well as receive. From her expression, it was plain she was trying to figure what she had to give. Then she got an idea and motioned to us to follow her outside.

Next to the house was an almost square cistern or reservoir of water. With both hands she first lifted a rusted tin cup off an old weathered wood cover and then pushed that aside. She almost prostrated herself on the ground to scoop water into the cup to give to me.

When I looked into the cistern, my stomach did flipflops. Several playing cards were floating in the water along with matchsticks and green slime.

"*Oh, no,*" I told myself. "*I can't drink that.*" Fascinated by the sickening filth of the water, I glanced at the expectant cherub-like face of Marta, her hand extended to me with the cup of water.

I was queasy. Yet if I turned down that cup of water, I would not only be rejecting Marta's gift of love, but Marta herself. Those large, expectant eyes looked up at me as I took the cup, thanked her and in the name of Jesus, claimed the promise of Mark 16:18 . . . and if they drink any deadly thing, it will not hurt them."

Somehow I gulped down the water, thinking that if it passed through my mouth and throat quickly it would contaminate me less. Chuck had seen the whole happening and stood in utter amazement but full understanding.

As I hugged Marta goodbye, and we entered the station wagon, Chuck said, "Charla, I never could have drunk that cup."

"Neither could I," I confesssed, "only in Jesus' name." And there was no sickness whatsoever.

On the following trip, I stopped again to see Marta and her sisters but the place was empty, abandoned. The mother and her family had moved. I have never seen them again and my mind keeps telling me what might have been for these lovely children and now what probably never will be.

But there was another kind of loss that saddened us and made us redouble efforts to keep it from happening again. Talk about a heartbreak — it is all I can do to keep from crying, even now.

On a hot August morning, I watched from the orphanage doorway as Ramiro, 15, and Francisco, 16, trudged down the dusty road, each with a sleeping bag and all earthly possessions in a brown paper sack.

They were on their own again — seven years older — re-entering a world that had become no less cold and indifferent with age.

I remembered the frightened, suspicious look of Ramiro at eight: his dark brown, curly hair, toast-colored skin, huge brown eyes and remarkably erect posture.

Francisco, at nine, had been dark and sullen but strikingly handsome, with blue-gray eyes and wavy, black hair. His chubby, four-year old sister Lupita followed him like a shadow.

They had lived through a nightmare that would never leave their memory: their father shooting their mother in front of them and then running as she moaned and bled to death. Ensenada police then shot him to death an hour later. Their grandmother could not take them in and nobody else wanted them. They were bed-wetters.

Ramiro and Francisco, both bright and talented,

became leaders of the children and excellent entertainers on the piano, bass fiddle and guitar, which they played beautifully by ear.

Now they had finished the equivalent of the eighth grade. Nowhere in the Guerrero area could they get additional schooling, although, within several years, we hoped to arrange that. With our advice, best wishes and prayers, they would go to Ensenada or Tijuana and make their own way. This was the best we could offer. None of the orphanage committee members was then financially free to devote full time to this project. So, through necessity we concentrated on the basics: providing shelter, clothing, food and a wholesome Christian environment.

As these gifted young men walked out of our lives, puffs of dust rising with each footstep, I cried out with a desolate heart:

"Oh, God, give us the vision and implementation to equip these, your children of promise, to face the future."

We orphanage committee members had often talked of searching mainland Mexico for Christian boarding schools to accommodate our talented young men and women — or at least Christian homes to board them while they attended one of the larger city preparatory (high) schools or trade schools.

In the former, they would prepare themselves for the university. In the latter, they could equip themselves for trades such as plumbing, auto repairing, carpentry, sheet metal work, nursing or bilingual secretarial service.

Some, of course, would go on to seminary to become evangelists to their people. Others would study to become doctors, lawyers, journalists or experts in petroleum or agriculture.

We prayed that some would enter government service and help govern their nation according to biblical principles.

Through churches, we followed many leads on mainland Mexico but were unable to find a Christian boarding school at the high school level or even Christian homes to board students.

Perhaps we would be forced to try Tijuana, where there was a good school. I shuddered. Tijuana, a cesspool of an environment, represented Mexico at its worst.

Yet we could not afford to let glowing potentials of our young people be snuffed out. We could not afford to lose more Ramiros and Franciscos.

22

MIRACLE OF THE FLOOD

The frightening darkness at noon was eerie. Angry jet-black clouds boiled in a strange titanic battle with steam-like gray and white ones as they swarmed in from the Pacific on the sticky, hot midday of August 16, 1977.

A rush of heavy raindrops flooded the windshield of my light blue Volkswagen, overmatching the old but reliable wipers.

Rain in southern California in August? It hadn't happened on that date since 1889, according to a newscast on the car radio. If I had listened carefully, I would have known that we were experiencing the forefront of Hurricane Dora.

Mary Hughes, a selfless Osborne Neighborhood Church worker and I, had just stopped in Chula Vista (near the border) to pick up Mary Lucero, a missionary friend, guide and interpreter for a day.

Our objective was to find in Tijuana a Christian boarding school or suitable Christian homes for our students hoping to enroll in preparatory or trade school.

Torrential rain and slides had covered Tijuana knee deep in dirty water, mud and rocks, through which we wallowed, following every lead. Soaked, bedraggled, forlorn, we finally had to give up. The sole Christian boarding school taught only through the eighth grade. No Christian homeowners seemed to have the room or the desire to house our students.

That morning I had prayed for success, and a Bible verse (Revelation 3:8) had almost lit up my mind: "I set before thee an open door. . .".

Weary, dejected, and uncommunicative, I drove the women back to Chula Vista and headed for Colonia Vicente Guerrero to let Bill and Kaye Lawrence know of our temporary setback. There was no way to reach them by phone.

In my soggy clothing, I shivered with cold. How wonderful it would have been to loll neck-deep in a hot bath! Darkness and violent rain did nothing to cheer me. What if the motor conked out or I had some other breakdown? Then I remembered Oswald Chambers' lines:

"The clouds are but the dust of our Father's feet. The clouds are a sign He is there."

What a comfort to know in dark clouds like the ones above me and trials, sorrow, bereavement — that *He cometh with clouds.*

The VW's headlight reflected on pools of water in the roadway. Peering through the streaming windshield and concentrating on the driving, I didn't realize until later that I had missed a sign at Manadero: "Road Closed."

Down into the blackness of the Santo Tomas valley, I did my best to hold the VW on the alleged road. Then in the headlights, I saw something that almost froze my heart — a landslide like a mountain, blocking the road.

Again through my mind flashed the verse, "I set before thee an open door!"

"This is an open door?" I asked myself. Something

urged me to get out of the VW and explore. Sure enough, I found a muddy shoulder of road. I felt uncomfortably close to a dropoff of 1,000 feet.

In the headlights under the persistent rain, I paced off the width of the shoulder and then the width of the VW. I felt a thrill. The measurements were almost the same! Still I tested the firmness of the shoulder. It was a long way down.

Then, as I got back in and inched the VW toward the shoulder, I heard the words and music of a sacred song:

"Got any rivers you think are uncrossable? Got any mountains you can't tunnel through? God specializes in things thought impossible. . .".

And now the VW and I squeaked through. Thank God I had not driven our wide station wagon that day!

Faith surged high. Now nothing would stop me. I had "mountain" faith.

Then, farther along, near Colonet, I peered out at a frightening sight. Torrential rains had turned a dry river basin into a raging flood and washed out the road. I had to get to the other side — about one hundred fifty feet away.

But how?

Once I had seen a flood like this carry a large tractor into the Pacific Ocean.

But God would not have opened one door to close another. He would have to part the flood waters like the Red Sea or get me over some other way. I had faith, not the usual kind, but supernatural faith.

In the enveloping darkness, I drove the car slowly into the waters. Possibly the road was only a foot or so underneath. I had no idea if the pavement had been washed out. As the VW splashed farther in, it became strangely bouyant.

I was afloat. Somewhere I had read that a VW will float. The motor continued smoothly and slowly, steadily the car glided ahead. Water began seeping through the floorboard. *Something incredible was happening.* Although the stream was moving quite strongly, the VW was not carried with it. Instead it was heading directly to where the road came up out of the water. As I neared the shore, the VW made a sloshing noise and lurched forward but it was nothing to fear. The tires had just made traction on the pavement.

Then the car was entirely out of the water right in the center of the road. Prayers of praise and thanks flowed almost unconsciously out of my mouth at this remarkable miracle.

Reaching the orphanage in the middle of the night, I rapped at the motel door of Inez' room. When she shook off her sleep and opened up, she stepped back startled. Inez couldn't believe what she saw.

"Charla, how did you get through? Nobody can get through. The road has been closed for 12 hours."

Then she realized I was really there, shivering from wet and cold and invited me in, still telling me that what had happened couldn't have happened.

"Why, Mr. Brown, our neighbor, tried to cross from this side with his 4-wheel drive and had to come back."

Inez gave me towels so I could dry off, made a cup of hot chocolate and put me into a warm bed. After I told her exactly what had taken place, we both believed more than ever that even the most extreme impossibility is possible with God.

Three years later I came to the same place during another disastrous flood. Roads and bridges had been washed out. Chuck and his buddy Rex Morningstar, a

Los Angeles County fireman, were stuck in Guerrero without boat or paddle. But I did not get a "drive ahead" from God and had to turn around and go home.

Why did God take the VW across the river one time and not another? Did I lack faith? I remembered a message given by Pastor Herb Mjorud on the subject of supernatural guidance. He explained the difference between two Greek words: logos and rhema. The logos is the recorded word of God from Genesis to Revelation. Rhema is God's word in specific circumstances. For instance, when Peter walked on the water it was in response to a rhema word from Jesus. "Come" and he went. But just because the account is written in the Bible does not mean henceforth and forevermore Christians will walk on water. Pastor Mjorud added that we must live in daily communion with God — taking each new situation as it comes — listening, trusting and obeying.

As I headed back to my home in North Hollywood I found myself singing, as I had so often before, "Trust and obey, for there's no other way, to be happy in Jesus, than to trust and obey."

God did provide a Christian home in Tijuana for our graduates from Guerrero. These young people needed a place to live while attending a preparatory school (high school) as the basis for a university education and professional career. We hope that shattering the eighth grade education barrier will offer a benefit over and above the direct help to individuals, an example for the entire Mexican orphanage system.

Our Tijuana home came about in a miraculous way, not according to our nearsighted plan but according to God's perfect plan. I always want things done right now but my mother has often said to me,

"Charla, God is not in a hurry!" One afternoon, still on a quest for the right dwelling, we found a huge, unfinished, adobe-block house for sale at $18,000 in a new residential area. It had a paved street, electric lights, sewer and even water piped in from the United States. Its location was ideal walking distance from the Technological School and The University of Tijuana. This two-story home with fourteen rooms and four baths seemed to have been specifically designed for our needs rather than for Tijuana home buyers. It was a white elephant on the market called "Ramon's Folly."

I was amazed to learn that Ramon had taken out a building permit to construct a four-room house on a significant date, August 16, 1977, the day Hurricane Dora did its best to do me in. For some reason, which Ramon himself did not understand, he kept adding rooms until he had "roomed" himself out of the usual market.

We needed a $10,000 down payment. Nova Nordseth, who had given us the key portion of our down payment on the orphanage property, received a personal investment payment of $10,000 and turned it over to us. Again Bill Riddell and his prayer group came through with money to buy building materials and more. Bill coordinated the building and labor and the house that nobody else wanted, soon was ready for occupancy.

Mark and Hanne Larson in Denmark read our appeal for houseparents in the Guerrero Newsletter. They called long-distance: "We would like to return to serve in Mexico when the house is ready."

The building inspector and Ramon had to sign the final papers transferring ownership but Ramon was nowhere to be found. All his neighbors said, "He took the money from his house and moved his small leather business to Guadalajara. We don't know where he is." I pleaded, "Does he have family here? A forwarding address?" They only gave a shrug of the shoulders and palms turned upward, a gesture understood as "I don't know" or "no se."

I mused, *"Surely, God, you haven't provided the house, the money, the laborers and houseparents for naught?"* I had a feeling that Ramon was somewhere in Tijuana, a city of two-and-a-half million people. *"I must find him!"*

After an exhausting and unfruitful day's search, I was driving through a busy intersection in Tijuana. Visibility was diminished by the rain and I drove into an open manhole. I got out of the car to survey my new predicament. The left front wheel was down to the axle. I felt like Jeremiah in the pit.

Drivers sped by, splashing me with muddy water and honking their horns. I cried, *"Oh, God, where is my help? Where is my deliverer?"* I put the jack in place and began lifting the car. A small boy came to my rescue. He asserted, "this is no job for a lady. I will help you." *Was this street urchin my deliverer?* I would rather have done the job myself. The boy looked into the open truck and spied Chuck's gloves, put them on his small hands and with an air of self-confidence, went to work. To my amazement the Chevy was soon out of the pit. As my little Good Samaritan was removing the huge gloves, I remembered that Ramon manufactured leather handball gloves. In my best "Spanglish" (Spanish and English mixed) I asked, "Do you know a man who makes gloves like these?"

"Si. Ramon. He lives down there."

I interjected, "Please take me to his house."

That evening I had Ramon's notorized signature on the legal documents. My help came from a little,

Spanish-speaking angel with a dirty face.

What a joy it is to see our Tijuana graduates making the breakthrough, reaching their goals as Christian professionals. It gives us faith for each new addition of children to our care.

23

END AND BEGINNING

Persistent, torrential rains can turn the usually arid Baja, California into a frightening nightmare. Innocent, dry river beds become frenzied, roaring streams — destroyers and killers — that overflow their banks and sweep away farmland, homes, roads, bridges and people.

That is what happened often in rainy seasons in 1977, 1978, 1979 and 1980. Sometimes it rains so hard for so long that, in moments of wavering faith, you wonder if God still remembers His promise after Noah's time never again to destroy life on earth by flood.

Frequently the raging waters have washed out the road and the bridge connecting Colonia Vicente Guerrero with the north.

Sometimes, as in 1978 and 1980, the village of Colonia V. Guerrero has been cut off from surface travel, like an island, with no means of coming or going except by airplane. During the 1980 storm, the river went wild and rampaging, even carving out a new course, sweeping away some huts and houses in the ejido and also a packing shed, crates of tomatoes, large out-buildings and farm machinery from Terry Tidmore, who leased 60 acres from us.

The spreading flood entered and polluted ground-level wells. God has always protected ours. It is on higher ground and sealed off from ground level water by an enclosing, small building with a deep base. Dave Taylor had emergency food and supplies flown down by the Orange County branch of the Christian Pilots Association. Committee members Paul and Marge Evans, who fly down monthly to supervise building construction, also delivered needed items.

When the boiling river changed course about a mile from our orphanage, it systematically sliced away land closer and closer to the small orphanage built ten years before by Willy.

Soldiers at the main road, at the southern approach to the bridge, saw that one of the buildings might soon be undermined and ordered the children and staff to evacuate the property immediately. Simultaneously the Delegado issued the same order.

Alerted to the danger, Chuck, a fireman friend, Rex Morningstar and male members of the staff — Anthony Arnold, Bill Rasch and Juan Carillo — drove to the road leading to the other orphanage and parked on high ground. Wading in the muck in waist-deep water, they made many trips, carrying thirty-seven children piggyback to safety.

As the roaring river shook the foundation of the building precariously perched on the bank, they moved out furniture, a stove, refrigerator, beds and mattresses.

On one of his trips into the building, Chuck noted an orange tree near the bank. Quickly he picked some fruit and then went inside for another load of furniture. When he came out, the tree was gone.

Already crowded to capacity, with new quarters still under construction, we housed the new children in the little church and in every spare corner that we could find. Their orphanage had been understaffed and poorly supported. Many of the children were malnourished, infested with lice and afflicted with impetigo and ring worm. Our staff, supplies, facilities and imaginations were taxed to serve them adequately.

My heart ached for these children. Like many of their predecessors, they lived under substandard conditions. The orphanage had not fully satisfied government standards since Willy had built it.

After Willy had been ordered to leave Mexico, several groups had tried unsuccessfully to re-establish the orphanage. The last person to make this effort was Cora Mendez, a Christian and an American who had married a Mexican and had run a child care center in Mexico City.

The high altitude contributed to a continuing heart ailment and doctors recommended that she move to a lower elevation. Six children in her care had been abandoned. She heard about the vacant Guerrero buildings, leased them and moved in with the children and then accepted others until the buildings were crowded.

In July of 1979, she died of a massive heart attack and left her son David and daughter-in-law Isabel and daughter Esther an unusual inheritance — 37 dependents with little support. David, 21 at the time, was a student at the Spanish language La Puente Bible Institute in Southern California, where he met and married Isabel. They and Esther felt it their Christian duty to run the orphanage.

David, called to be a pastor, felt ill-equipped and inadequate to direct an orphanage. Then the flood came and destroyed much of the orphanage that Willy had built out of division and contention, a project void of God's glory. Perhaps it was for the best so far as the children were concerned, because the orphanage was out of money and support.

David and Isabel requested that we permit them to merge with us. Our committee of the FOUNDATION FOR HIS MINISTRY Mission at Colonia Vicente Guerrero held a special meeting and voted in favor of the merger. We asked David to be the pastor of our small congregation of staff, children and neighbors.

For fourteen years we had labored in Colonia Guerrero, caring for many children but without seeing the fulfillment of the great harvest of souls seen in the vision on our first trip in October, 1966. Through David's ministry we have seen the first fruits of the harvest. We are not just an orphanage but have officially come to be know as a mission.

24

GOD PAVES THE WAY

Isaiah 45:2 says, "I will go before you and make the rough places smooth. . . . I will shatter the doors of bronze and cut through their iron bars."

Many times on the monotonous, exhausting journey to Colonia Vicente Guerrero, I pray and thank God for turning the vision of Pastor Brody and myself into reality through a combination of His miracles, the generosity of many donors and hard work.

One of God's amazing miracles was right under my tires, the paved road from Ensenada to Guerrero, which slashed my one-way travel time to seven hours. There was no way that road improvement could have happened solely through human efforts.

After making the fourteen-hour drive for a number of years, I was asked by a Lutheran pastor, "Charla, how long does it take you to drive those last thirty-eight rugged miles?"

"About four hours."

"What do you do during those four hours, Charla?"

"What do you mean, what do I do? I watch the road for chuckholes."

He was incredulous. "Are you telling me that on

"X" number of trips, four hours each way, you haven't prayed that God would pave the road?"

I had prayed about everything but that. He was right. I had been tolerating the wretched road, rather than giving the problem to God. So those of us who made the trip frequently, actually our whole community and friends, made this a prayer project. It was the year of the Olympic Games in Mexico City and all tax dollars were being funneled to improve mainland roads so that more people would attend. Baja officials told us that the odds were astronomical against our road *ever* being paved. Just when external circumstances did their best to discourage our prayers, road construction machinery and materials moved in and paving of a new, smooth, safe road was started and finished.

Two lessons grew out of that experience: even the most astronomical of odds can't stand up against God and the road to Guerrero was paved with prayer.

Passage of goods across the border from the United States into Mexico is impossible without endless red tape. Letters must be signed in three different offices in Tijuana and Ensenada. "Mordida" (bribes) are paid at the border. But God gave us a rhema word at the inception of our ministry that, "a bribe is a mockery to your God." Thus, in this too, we are dependent on God to open the doors in answer to the prayer of faith.

In 1982 the medfly, a tiny insect, infested southern California. All shipment of fruit was stopped either by boycott or quarantine. Tons of fruit were dumped on the Mojave Desert.

I received a call from George Voita, a young enterprising wholesale fruit broker. "Charla, can you use some oranges in Mexico?"

"Oh, George," I exclaimed, "we never have enough fresh fruit!"

"Come and get all you can carry. They are rotting here on the dock."

As the last of fifty boxes were being loaded into the van, George looked quizzically at me and asked, "Charla, how are you going to get this load across the border?"

"I can't," I answered, "but God can!"

As we were nearing the border the iron gateway and the letters M-E-X-I-C-O came into view. Denny, our son-in-law who was riding along, asked a rhetorical question: "Mother, how do we pray today?"

"How do *you* think we should pray?" I asked him.

"I think we had better pray for a border guard who has no sense of smell," he replied. "I don't think they will have to look in the truck because these oranges are so ripe he will smell us coming — we smell like an Orange Julius on wheels!"

We crept to a halt, sixth in a long line of cars waiting to cross the border. Apprehension was crowding faith into a dark corner. Usually, passenger vehicles were waved through without being stopped. The driver of the car in front of us was told to get out and open his trunk for inspection while another officer looked under the auto. In times like these, one's lofty prayers to the God of the universe are reduced to one word, "Jesus!" The guard motioned for us to drive into the secondary inspection area which meant we would have to unload our precious sweet cargo. Since we were on Mexican soil the oranges could be confiscated. I got down from the driver's seat and walked slowly but directly to the "officina" of the "heffe" (office of the Chief). He was not there. His replacement happened to be the only federal border official I knew. Faith emerged triumphant over fear. He greeted me with an endearing title, "Hermana!" which means sister. "Go right by!" I thanked him sincerely and also thanked the Lord Jesus. He had done it again!

The incident so astonished George Voita that after I relayed the story to him he said, "I will furnish your children with all the oranges they need until Jesus comes again." He has been faithful to that promise even though the cost is great.

Since eggs are almost as scarce as hens' teeth on the menu at our mission, the offer of one-hundred young laying hens was received with much enthusiasm. We had one problem: how do you get noisy hens across the border? We could cover the cages but how do you stop the infernal cackling?

Our truck driver picked up the chickens, five to a cage, in Orange County, about thirty-five miles south of Los Angeles. Just before crossing the border, he covered the cages with a tarpaulin and a prayer. "Peace be still." He drove the truck into the commercial vehicle inspection area and gave the border guard the letter-permit with the hope and prayer that the inspection would be waived. But it wasn't.

The guard told him to open the rear door. He stepped down from the cab of the truck, dreading the outcome of the next moments. He walked slowly to the rear and reluctantly opened the door. Standing aside to watch the guard, he was astonished by what he saw. The guard wore earphones and was listening to a pocket radio! He couldn't hear the cackling chickens, Hallelujah! The guard looked but did not see and motioned for the trucker to continue on his way.

On two other occasions God provided miraculous passage for chickens. Once a guard was so distracted by questioning a typographical error in our permit-letter that he didn't bother to look in the truck! (Cluck, cluck)

OUTREAC

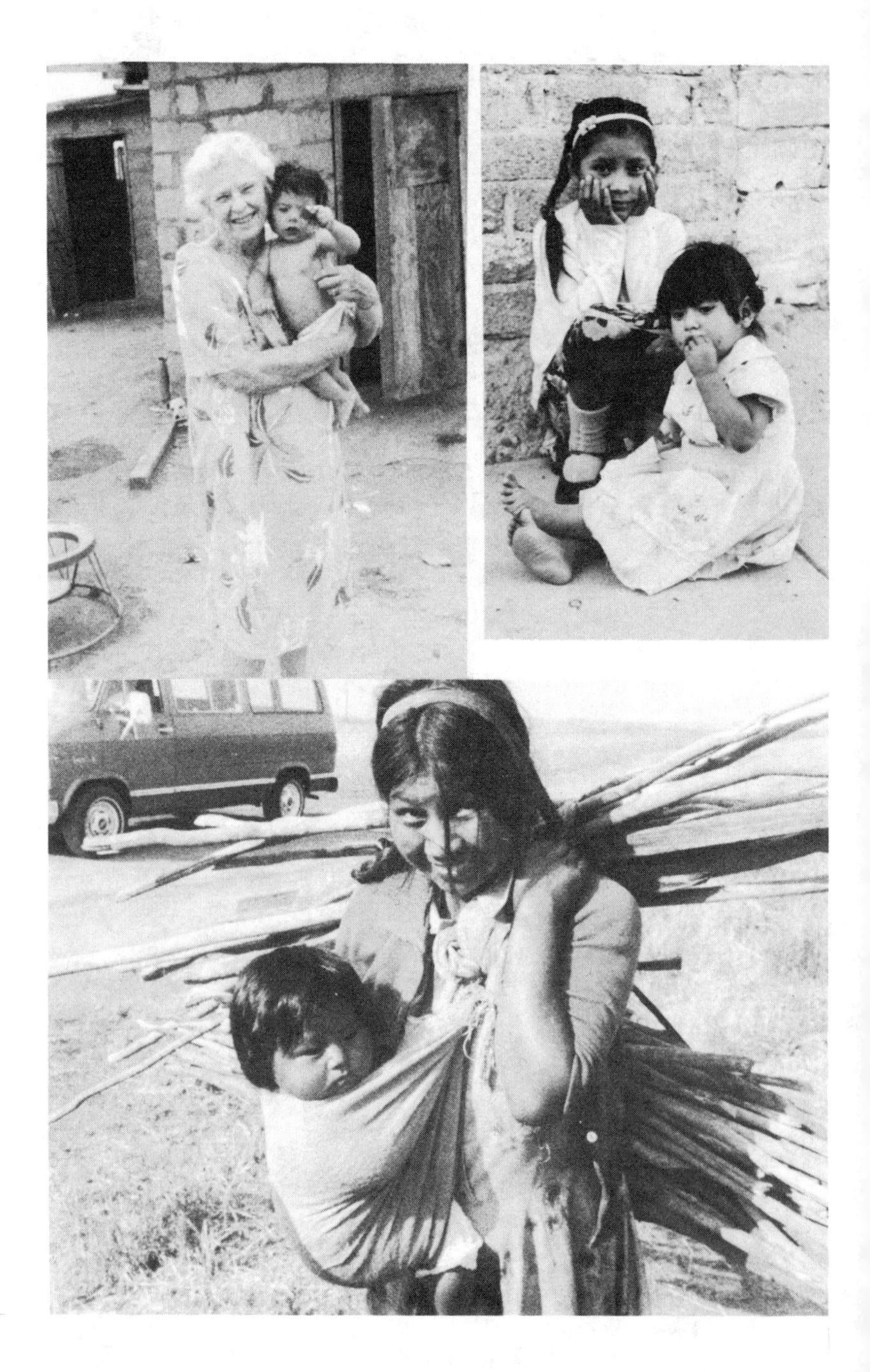

Part of our Outreach Team

25

THE MASTER'S PLAN

Throughout the years, Jean Darnall's prophecy from Isaiah 58, given before the property in Mexico was purchased, has been a recurring theme. This ancient prophecy from the Old Testament continues to unfold as God brings into being His will for the Mission.

vs. 6 *Is this not the fast which I chose,*
To loosen the bonds of wickedness,
To undo the bands of the yoke,
And to let the oppressed go free
And break every yoke?

The original purpose for the land and buildings where the Mission now stands was to provide the services of a casino and brothel to rich Americans visiting nearby Hamilton Ranch. This center of iniquity created an atmosphere of corruption that hung over the site until spiritual house-cleaning freed the land from ominous darkness.

Our splendid facility stands as a wonderful testimony to His faithfulness. It's a home for about eighty of His little ones. Built by volunteer labor and paid for by widows' mites, it was dedicated on Pentecost Sunday, 1981.

vs 7 *Is it not to divide your bread with the hungry*

And bring the homeless poor into the house,
When you see the naked, to cover him;
And not to hide yourself from your own flesh?

When Jean gave this prophecy, she placed a heavy emphasis on the King James translation that refers to bringing the poor into *thy* house. The message was the go-ahead to purchase the land in Mexico. The prophecy hit home with the reference to *your own flesh.* We have felt intimately connected to the people of Mexico through the adoption of two sons . . . one Mexican, the other Oaxacan . . . into our own family.

On more than one occasion as we have divided our bread with the hungry we have seen a miraculous multiplication of our food.

Unni Svendsen from Norway, working in our soup kitchen reported, "Dere yust vasn't enough soup to feed so many people, but I yust gave and gave and da pot vas not empty until every von had all dey vanted."

Yet my faith so often wavers. There are times when I enter the double doors of the dining room and see before me a sea of faces. I see over a hundred and twenty staff and children chattering, laughing and praying. I back out, overwhelmed with my responsibility.

The adversary whispers, "They are all dependent on you for their daily bread."

Hit by this wave of despondency — I cry out to the Lord, *"How can I possibly provide for the needs of these little ones?"*

Then I lift up my eyes to the beautiful mountains to the East of us and ask, as the Psalmist did, *"From whence shall my help come? . . . My help comes from the Lord God who is the Father to the fatherless."*

It is His responsibility, not mine.

Dividing our bread goes even beyond those children living at the home. Revival has come to the Baja. We are currently involved in an intense program of evangelism, discipleship and mercy ministry to thousands of destitute, migrant Oaxacan Indians who labor in the fields around our facility. In addition to feeding and caring for our Mission family, we are stretching out to almost 10,000 of these needy Indians who number about 40,000 in all. In the name of our Lord Jesus we offer them a monthly clothes allotment, weekly food portion and provision of basic medical and education assistance. Our doctor and nurse have rarely a spare second!

Through the extensive use of various media techniques (videos in our free soup kitchen and films out in the camps), we have witnessed an incredibly positive response to the preaching of the Gospel. They have filled our little church to overflowing and we have had to begin construction of a new 800-seat worship center.

vs. 8 *Then your light will break out like the dawn,*
And your recovery will speedily spring forth
And your righteousness will go before you.
The glory of the Lord will be your rear guard

This verse has been of special significance to me. My personal health has undergone a radical improvement since my involvement in this project. Ten years of major sickness and repeated hospitalization gave way to twenty years of perfect health with only three colds. Hundreds of trips to Mexico with its unsanitary conditions and countless hours of moving heavy boxes and furniture in my garage have not affected the good health that God has granted.

The light breaking out like dawn referred to here has been seen on two separate occasions as a supernatural light over the grounds of the Mission, a testimony to God's hand on the work done in His name there.

vs. 9 *Then you will call and the Lord will answer;*
You will cry and He will say, "Here I am."
If you will remove the yoke from your midst,
The pointing of the finger, and speaking wickedness.

Through the many conflicts that are inevitable in an organization like ours, God has commanded that we never point fingers or speak wickedness. The temptations to defend ourselves must be resisted if God's blessings are to flow among us.

In 1985 we had a short dispute among our staff in Guerrero. There was backbiting and a division unbeknown to our donors. Yet, our financial contributions which are usually good in the spring dwindled to less than half of minimal operating expenses. In times like this there are three rhetorical questions I ask:

1. Are we in the will of God?
2. Is the provision within the camp?
3. Is there sin in the camp?

The latter was obviously true. We called John Lucas of Canada, our spiritual advisor and asked him to come and minister to the staff. After a time of fasting, prayer and teaching we experienced a breaking, genuine repentance, confession, reconciliation and rejoicing. The windows of heaven opened and God poured out His blessings through a wide diversity of donors.

Day 1 (Monday) - We received a check for \$14,100.28 from a woman in Cedar Rapids, Iowa. This was her first contribution. The accompanying note gave the following explanation. "I received your newsletter the same day I received a check from an investment. God seemed to say *give it all.*"

Day 2 (Tuesday) - A friend in Chicago, Illinois, purchased a *NEW* van for our outreach ministry. ($13,000)

Day 3 (Wednesday) - The president of the Niles Rotary called to tell me they were sending a sixty-eight passenger diesel bus completely reconditioned inside and out.

Day 4 (Thursday) - Jim Bronson of Costa Mesa, California, had an almost new commercial dishwasher for us.

Day 5 (Friday) - Reap International gave us desperately needed medical equipment for the clinic.

Day 6 (Saturday) - The councilmen for the City of Los Angeles offered a paramedic unit which they no longer used.

Day 7 (Sunday) - God rested.

Vs. 10 *And if you give yourself to the hungry,*
And satisfy the desire of the afflicted,
Then your light will rise in darkness,
And your gloom will become like midday.

As we comply with God's command to care for the hungry and afflicted, He is faithful in bringing light to the darkness. Throughout the years His guidance of our steps has been miraculous and very specific in situations where solutions seemed impossible.

Lucio, which means light, lay helpless on a desolate beach. He had been shot in the head and left for dead. Some unknown samaritan took the lifeless body to the little Baptist hospital near San Quintin. He lived, but the light of his mind and eyes was snuffed out. The plight of a sixteen year old boy without sight or the ability to reason is hopeless in Mexico.

The clinic placed him under the guardianship of Pastor David Mendez. He taught Lucio to sweep the church by pushing a large broom along the walls. He also learned to sweep the patio. The staff and children prayed daily for Lucio.

About a year later, little messengers came running with the good news . . . "Lucio can see! Lucio can see!" One of the children had seen him bend over, pick up a piece of cardboard and use it for a dustpan.

God restored Lucio's mind and his eyesight. Lucio gave public testimony to God's amazing grace . . . "I was lost, but now am found; was blind, but now I see."

Lucio, a light in the darkness, later went back to his home in the mainland of Mexico.

vs. 11 *And the Lord will continually guide you,*
And satisfy your desire in scorched places,
And give strength to your bones;
And you will be like a watered garden,
And like a spring of water whose waters do not fail.

He *IS* satisfying our desire to see both physical and spiritual renewal in the scorched places of the San Quintin Valley where only three inches of rain falls annually. One of our favorite blessings of all has been the emergence of an oasis in the desert. In 1966 the establishment of a watered garden in the area seemed impossible. Today our experimental orchard houses hundreds of exotic fruits and nuts that have been grown, grafted and developed into miracles that have attracted horticulturalists from as far away as Israel, who come to see the wonders of our oasis.

Through years of drought and water shortage, when neighboring wells have run dangerously low, our water level has never been seriously affected. During a particularly dry season, the possibility of conservation of water was considered. Restricting water to personal use only would have meant letting the garden and orchard dry up and die. But because of this verse, we made the faith decision to continue to water the grounds. Our spring of water did not fail. God has promised that it never will.

God promises strength and after 520 trips to Colonia Guerrero, which is the equivalent to driving more than fourteen times around the earth, and countless miles during deputation, I can attest to the fact that He has.

vs. 12 *And those from among you will rebuild the ancient ruins:*
You will raise up the age-old foundations:
And you will be called the repairer of the breach.
The restorer of the streets in which to dwell.

The original Board of Directors was made up from a prayer group which still meets at our home on Friday night. These friends took on the task of rebuilding the ruins of a 1920's casino and brothel into a Home for Needy Children. Then God sent other skilled builders with servants hearts: Anthony Arnold, from British Columbia, Canada; Chuck Mills, a mason from Portland, Oregon; Harold Craig, an electrician from Three Hills, Alberta, Canada; Jim Bronson, master plumber from Costa Mesa, California, to name but a few.

The restoration referred to in this verse speaks of streets — our property fronts on two roads. How specific.

vs. 13 *If because of the Sabbath, you turn your foot,*
From doing your own pleasure on My holy day,
And call the Sabbath a delight, the holy day of the Lord honorable
And shall honor it, desisting from your own ways,

From seeking your own pleasure,
And speaking your own word.

Here God reaffirms His commandment to keep a day of rest holy and set apart for Him. Is it odd that we must be commanded to *REST*? Not if you are a Type A personality and are in a hurry, therefore think God must also be in a hurry, and value productivity.

More often than not I crawl into bed exhausted, breathe in and exhale a prayer, *"Thank you God for my bed. I sure earned my keep today."* I pondered where that colloquial expression came from. A scene from earliest childhood came to mind. Joyously greeting my dad as he came home from work, he would jokingly ask my mother, "Did this little one earn her keep?"

I must continually and carefully re-examine my priorities, reserving or scheduling time for meditation on the Scripture, for prayer, for interaction with other believers, for worship. It was Jesus who said, "If you know these things, happy are ye if you do them."

vs.14 *Then you will take delight in the Lord,*
And I will make you ride on the heights of the earth,
And I will feed you with the heritage of Jacob your father,
For the mouth of the Lord has spoken.

In the light of His love and faithfulness to me, I surely do take delight in the Lord.

Prior to becoming involved in His Ministry in Mexico my only airplane trip was to pick up Charles Curtis in San Antonio, Texas on November 9, 1961. Today I ride on the heights of the earth throughout the United States, Canada and Europe ministering, teaching and sharing the wonderful works of God.

The adventures I have had traveling, representing Jesus and His Ministry, could and will doubtless fill another book.

He continues to fulfill His prophecy today and I trust in Him for our future for "the mouth of the Lord has spoken". Hallelujah!

THE MISSION

OUTREACH CENTER
ORIGINAL
BUILDINGS
THE CLINIC
CHILDRENS' HOME

Epilogue

Over the years I told Charles Curtis many things about his past: how God brought him to us, how his mother loved him so much that she gave him up — a part of herself — for his good, and how he had always been a blessing to our family.

When he was seven years old we took him to Guerrero. Fifty children sat at long tables, eating and conversing in rapid Spanish. As he, Chuck and I sat down, he could hardly take his eyes off the children.

"Where are their fathers and mothers?" he asked me.

"They have none," I replied. "Some of the children's parents have been killed. Some of their mothers have been deserted by their fathers and can't find work to support their children."

He glanced up into my face.

"Mother, why doesn't somebody adopt them?" he asked, earnestly.

I caught my breath, then sighed, not knowing how to answer. Most of our children were not adoptable — no birth certificate, no legal documents and it involved horrendous red tape to anyone who wanted to try to adopt a child. I remembered back to the Charla Pereau who didn't want to upset her comfortable lifesytle by adopting an Indian baby. I wondered, "*How many people really care?*"

Charles Curtis seemed to understand what it meant to be adopted. As we were about to leave, one of the orphanage staff members laughed and jokingly asked:

"Why don't you leave Charles Curtis with us? He fits in beautifully."

An expression of terror crossed Charles Curtis' face and he ran to Chuck, wrapping his arms around his father's legs.

When he was in first grade, something happened which made me realize how adopted children who are loved become an integral part of a family. He was unhappy when he had come home from school with a note from his teacher saying he needed an eye examination. When he took it, results showed that he had astigmatism. That night I mentioned this to Chuck who had come into the kitchen. His comment: "How can that be? Nobody in the Pereau family or your family has ever had to wear glasses."

"You've got to be kidding, Chuck!" I exclaimed. Then I realized he was not. He had made the slip because Charles Curtis was no longer just Charles Curtis. He had truly become Charles Curtis Pereau.

This made me think about how, in a similar manner, God lets us become grafted into His family. God forgets what we have been and what we have done when we invite His Son, Jesus, into our hearts and lives. Then we are a permanent member of His family. He forgets that this was not always so, just as Chuck did with Charles Curtis Pereau.

With the expansion of and the growing interest in the mission, I am often invited by churches, Christian organizations or service clubs to tell the story of how God used ordinary people to do an extraordinary work. The story I am most often requested to tell is that of my personal struggle taking in and adopting an Indian baby from Oaxaca, Charles Curtis.

Never will I forget how at age two-and-one-half he brought home the Sunday School paper with a drawing of a boy, a dog, and the sun with the caption, "Look what God has done for me." That day I thanked God for this beautiful child and His amazing grace, and rededicated Charles Curtis and myself to the Lord. In the sequel to *Charla's Children* I will share the nightmarish saga of the years Curtis was enslaved to alcohol, his deliverance, and the amazing story of how God brought his natural mother back into our lives.

Without my knowing Charles Curtis and later Greg, I might never have broken out of my Radford Avenue cloister and learned how to love an expanded family. I would have missed the joy of caring for hundreds of other "Charles Curtises" rescued from the slavery of abject poverty, illiteracy and the curse of disease and high mortality.

Too few are willing to deny self and take up his or her cross daily and follow wherever He leads. The greatest sacrifice I've been required to make is not financial, hard work, or long hours, but time away from our children and grandchildren. The rhema word given to us by Pastor Percy Gutteridge so long ago, "You take care of mine and I will take care of yours," is a conditional covenant we have claimed. I have prayed that God the Father would compensate in some way and give them grace and understanding.

Today, *Andrea* lives in the desert community of Lancaster, California, with her husband Denny Lombard. Denny works for Lockheed Aircraft as a technical photographer. They have two daughters and all are active in their church. When Andrea read the first edition of *Charla's Children* she phoned me and said, "Now I understand you, Mother."

Dana, a supervisor in the loss prevention business, has a lovely home in Whittier, California, with his wife Sharon and two children. He and Sharon both served for a time with "Youth With a Mission" in Europe and Cypress.

Craig, a fine tree surgeon for the City of Los Angeles, and his wife Loree, an escrow title officer, have two children. They live in North Hollywood and love to visit the mission.

Charles Curtis, a driver for Gelson's markets, and his wife Lisa have two children. They live in North Hollywood and also are active at Osborne Neighborhood Church.

My mind recoils at what might have happened to little Rosa and Angel who are doing well. *Angel,* thanks to God and his benefactors, went through many operations over the years and gets around well on crutches. He is on staff at Rancho Santa Marta in San Vicente, Mexico, doing auto painting and body work. *Rosa* is married and she works as a supervisor for the telephone company in Mexico City. I was deeply touched when she and her husband named their first born Charla after me.

Dave and Audrey Taylor of Costa Mesa retired from the board June 1984 after years of voluntary service, he as chairman of the board and she as newsletter editor.

Inez Sorenson is caring for her sister in Redwood Falls, Minnesota. However, we never know when she's going to pop up as she did in Oregon-Illinois, looking quite fashionable in her latest creation.

Mark Larson is on staff at World Vision. *Hanne* is housemother at a home for troubled young people.

The *Klanckes* still are in their Garden Grove home. Harold is now confined to a wheelchair, but his spirit is with us. Our former treasurer scrutinizes our every financial report. Ruth continues to send precious notes of encouragement.

The *Beans,* who made that first unforgettable trip with us to Colonia Guerrero, still serve as directors on our board. Roy has a ministry to and with alcoholics at the Church on the Way in Van Nuys.

Max Christian joined our staff in 1980. At my first meeting with this bright young man, who came to us as a short-term volunteer, I had one of those inner-knowings that one day he would be our mission administrator. In all his dealings he manifests Christ-like character. His service has been diversified: buildings and grounds maintenance, housefather to our young boys then a family group. He has implemented sportsnight and camping programs open to the community. God raised him up from among us.

Our good friend *Dr George Wood* of Costa Mesa gave a formula for failure in his teaching on the feeding of the five thousand: "Look at the size of the task, the little you have, and leave Jesus out of the picture."

FOUNDATION FOR HIS MINISTRY
BOX 9803
NORTH HOLLYWOOD, CA 91609

CANADIAN ADDRESS:
MARANATHA EVANGELISTIC ASSOCIATION
P.O. BOX 1292
CALGARY, ALBERTA, CANADA T2P 2L2